SCOTTISH EDUCATION DEPARTMENT

Issues in
Educational Assessment

D0715339

Edinburgh
Her Majesty's Stationery Office

I SBN 0 11 491606 3

CONTENTS

THE CONTRIBUTORS

Sandy Jeffrey	HMI Secondary Education with special responsibility for assessment
Dr Brian Dockrell	Director of the Scottish Council for Research in Education
Dr Sally Brown	Senior Research Fellow, Education Department, Stirling University
Dr Albert Pilliner	Former Director of the Godfrey Thomson Unit for Academic Assessment, University of Edinburgh
Alastair Pollitt	Assistant Director of the Godfrey Thomson Unit, University of Edinburgh
Dr David Walker	Former Director of the Scottish Council for Research in Education
Ernest Spencer	Research Officer at the Scottish Council for Research in Education
James Gillam	Senior Examinations Officer and Statistician, SCEEB
Dr Stuart Kellington	Senior Lecturer in Physics at Notre Dame College of Education
Bart McGettrick	Assistant Principal, Notre Dame College of Education
Bob Weir	HMI Western Division, Music Specialist

The Scottish Education Department invited articles from the above contributors, but the views expressed are necessarily their own.

FOREWORD

Assessment or, in the narrower sense, tests and examinations, have always been part of schooling. Indeed, so much a part of education have they become and so important have they seemed to pupils that even the habitual absentees turn up to school and present themselves for the examinations. Teachers, and indeed the whole education system, have both been accused, sometimes with good reason, of being examination dominated. While the quality of examinations set by the Scottish Certificate of Education Examination Board is probably as high as it is possible to obtain, the same cannot always be said for the various assessment instruments prepared by teachers in our schools; the considerable expertise in curriculum development which many teachers have acquired in the last 10 or 15 years has not been paralleled by a similar growth in the ability to prepare valid, reliable tests to measure with reasonable precision, all the effects on pupils produced by the new syllabuses upon which they have laboured so intensively.

In recent years many people have made efforts, particularly in America, to specify as precisely as possible the objectives of various courses of study which make up the curriculum. This has served partly to clarify to both teacher and pupil exactly what the course is about, partly to facilitate the preparation of programmed learning packages, either in printed or computer programme form. Such specification has not only affected the nature of courses and methodologies used to present them, but out of it has arisen a whole new concept, the idea of mastery learning and, coupled with it, the new field of criterion-referenced and domain-referenced testing. Such tests measure pupil achievement relative to the objectives to be achieved, rather than the more usual form of norm-referenced test which measures pupil performance relative to other pupil performances. This in turn has required a new approach to the statistical analysis of the results of such tests; such problems have not yet been fully resolved.

Although the idea of stating clear objectives for courses of study is not new, Tyler was suggesting it in 1950, it was not readily accepted. Bloom's *Taxonomy*, published in 1956, was no more successful in its early years than Tyler had been, and it was only in the early 1960's that the growth in interest began in earnest and the first signs of the exponential nature of this growth became evident. At about the same time Georg Rasch was speculating about an alternative method of categorising the relative difficulty of test items and the ability of students to answer them. Out of this speculation came the new concept of latent trait modelling. With the possibility of calculating item difficulties which are sample free and of measuring student abilities which are test free, it became possible to conceive of banks of test items, based on a single calibration, for each element of the curriculum. Such banks would be available for testing students of all levels of ability and of all ages. What Rasch first saw as a statistical principle applicable to questions which could be marked either right or wrong has since been extended so that it can encompass questions for which there are several answers of different degrees of correctness. This extends still further the range of test items which can be banked and increases the subject areas for which some form of banking is feasible.

At about the time that these ideas could be said to have achieved widespread if not total acceptance, James Munn's Committee produced a report 'The Curriculum in The Third and Fourth Years in Scottish Secondary Schools' and Joe Dunning's Committee produced another 'Assessment for All' for the same group. Both are published by HMSO. Munn recommended, amongst many other things, a differentiated curriculum at 3 levels, with transfer between levels possible for as long as possible. Dunning recommended certification for all, the use of continuous assessment and the need to use criterion-referenced tests particularly with the lowest or Foundation level courses. His report also suggests the use of procedures for reporting on pupils in the form of a profile of performance which should include the description of certain attitudes as well as the attainment in a variety of cognitive skills.

Since we seem to be on the threshold of the next major advance in Scottish education it seemed worthwhile to consider how some of the more recent developments in the field of assessment might relate to the changes which Munn and Dunning may occasion. To this end, and to clarify its own thinking, HM Inspectorate in Scotland has asked a small group of people, expert in their own fields, to contribute a paper each on an aspect of assessment of present interest and a further group to discuss how these and other techniques might be applied in assessing certain areas of the curriculum. The opinions expressed in these papers are the authors' own, and do not represent any official, Departmental viewpoint. The papers are of high quality and are so stimulating that the Inspectorate believe they should be read much more widely. They have therefore made them available in this Occasional Paper in the hope that they will prove to the wider audience as useful a starting point for discussions on assessment as they have done to the Inspectorate.

A.W.J.

In recent years accountability has become a matter of concern in many countries. The Education Commission of the States (ECS) has as its major project in the USA the National Assessment of Educational Progress (NAEP). The principal function of this organisation since 1969 has been to gather information concerning the extent to which educational goals are being met nationally and to publish this information so that those responsible can identify problems, establish priorities and effect necessary changes. Continuing monitoring can then show changes over time. The publication in 1975 of the first report on Mathematics, for example, revealed that only a very small proportion of 17 year olds and adults could either balance a cheque book or compute a taxi fare. Steps have been taken to correct such failings in social arithmetic. Most of the States in the Union also monitor over a wide range of ages and subject areas. In 1974 The Assessment of Performance Unit, an organisation with similar functions, was set up within the Department of Education and Science in England. Several other countries in the Commonwealth and in Europe have similar organisations with similar functions. The Dunning Report suggested that Scotland also should carry out national monitoring and this suggestion received support from several bodies in their submissions to the Secretary of State on that report.

Here Dr Brian Dockrell, who is Director of the Scottish Council for Research in Education, recounts that the idea is not new, that in one guise or another it has been going on in Scotland for many years, and gives examples of the results obtained. He also casts doubts on the claims that are sometimes made for the benefits to education that may flow from such assessment. This should give us pause for thought.

While some would take a different view about some of the points which Dr Dockrell raises in his paper it is necessary for all of us to bear in mind both sides, and equally necessary for the proponents of monitoring to provide the cogent counter arguments about standards, about relevance, and about potential benefit, if their viewpoint is to carry the day when the time comes to decide whether or not we should undertake continuous national monitoring in Scotland.

A.W.J.

A*

1

National Surveys of
Achievement

W. B. Dockrell

My original intention had been to call this article 'Why, What and How' until I discovered that the English Assessment of Performance Unit had produced a leaflet with just that title. To use the title would be plagiarism but to use the basic structure is I think legitimate.

The notion of national surveys of attainments is a familiar one for Scots. The first of the scholastic surveys (Scottish Scholastic Survey, SCRE, 1963) was carried out in 1953 when tests of English and Arithmetic were administered to over 72,000 ten year olds. The survey faced all the fundamental questions. Why should a survey be carried out? 'To indicate the amount of acceleration and retardation in the school system, the relative educational standards of urban and rural schools of different sizes of schools and of schools organised on individual as compared with class methods'.

The question of what was to be tested was not given much space in the final report. It was originally intended that only Arithmetic should be included in the survey. However, it was decided to take advantage of the opportunity to include English as well. At that date the inclusion of Arithmetic (mechanical and reasoning) and English (usage and comprehension) was apparently self evident and did not need to be justified.

The 'how' question was answered equally simply. It was to be administered to all pupils born between the 5 July 1942 and the 30 June 1943.

The conclusions from this original survey are also instructive. 'In the first place it has been shown that a scholastic survey on a national scale is possible with the goodwill of teachers and administrators.' That in itself is important since 25 years later there are still a number of countries where no national survey has been attempted and where there is considerable doubt about the feasibility of such surveys. 'But the survey has also shown the difficulties of which the principal one is the diversity of work normally professed by an age group. At the ten year old level chosen for the survey this was particularly evident in the subject of Arithmetic where the complicated British tables of money, length and weight were introduced in different ways at different times in different areas. It will be folly to attempt to standardise curricula in this field until it has been shown that one method is superior to others'. This quotation highlights two issues for those wishing to attempt national surveys today. The first is the great variation in attainments in subjects which reflect not long term differences in level of attainment but short term consequences of different teaching methods. The second is the danger of a backwash in the schools. If there are standard examinations which are to be administered nationally it may be assumed that these define a national curriculum in the way that the examinations of the examination board define a national curriculum. Schools will be under pressure to adopt this putative 'national curriculum'. This is a fundamental issue which is discussed in more detail later.

These difficulties did not prevent the panel reaching definite conclusions. They list them as follows:

1. 'Division by factors is undesirable in the primary schools.

2. More attention should be paid to the layout of the short division sums.

3. There is need for standardising the notation used in recording the time of day

by the clock. The panel recommends that for written expression it should be in the form 8.50 a.m.

4. Use of written working in Arithmetic facilitates accuracy. Further use of working is helpful to a teacher in diagnosing a pupil's difficulties . . .

5. A standard practice is required for recording remainders in division . . .

6. The final point on Arithmetic to be mentioned here is partly a question of the use of English. It was evident that the various aspects of teaching arithmetical problems required further consideration *e.g.* the need for accurate reading of the question and for noting units used'.

The panel dealing with the English tests arrived at equally definite conclusions:

1. 'The tests in English usage demonstrated the need for persistent oral practice in accepted speech forms' and a restrained use of pencil and paper exercises for occasional testing . . .

2. Reading as a thought-getting process seemed insecure. It is possible that acquaintance with the forms of verbal testing and the common use of reading text books with exercises make it all too easy to suppose that pupils working through a series of questions have understood what they are reading. The tests in this survey showed unmistakcably that many pupils dealing as well as they could with details have not first grasped the general meaning of what they had read . . .

These curricular comments are derived from an analysis of the tests. What is to be noted is that they refer to general teaching procedures. They are meant as a guidance to teachers in the schools about the practices that they should follow.

By 1963 there was more sophistication in the 'how'—the research design. Indeed there is a whole chapter on experimental design which focuses on such questions as sampling. By this time it was recognised that a sample would provide as reliable information as testing of the whole population so rather fewer than 5,000 pupils were tested instead of the earlier 72,000. What is more, this was a stratified random sample representative of cities, large towns, small towns and other areas and grant-aided and independent schools. Within the strata were drawn samples from schools of different sizes. There is a lengthy and sophisticated discussion of the merits of random sampling and cluster sampling and an explanation of why cluster sampling was preferred.

In the later text, (Rising Standards in Scottish Primary Schools, SCRE, 1968), the conclusions were fewer and simpler: 'Periodical survey of this type serve a useful purpose giving teachers, administrators and the public some assessment of the products of primary education and enabling comparisons to be made over the years. . . . Each survey also gives teachers some indication of the strengths and weaknesses of pupils in the basic skills. In order that any teacher who so desires may find how her pupils compare with the Scottish averages the committee recommends the tests used in this survey be made available for purchase by teachers'.

Some of these conclusions are general and refer to changes in scores that took place in the intervening ten years. The study looks not only at general differences. The changes are related also to levels of ability, sex, types of area, region, sizes of schools, aspects of the tests and so on. Some of them are more specific and relate to the retention of attainment tests in some areas, use of the cuisenaire method, the provision of libraries in schools, the effects of shortages of teachers, length of schooling and left-handedness. These indicate the kind of questions that a survey of this kind may attempt to answer. The general question was answered in the title of the book, 'Rising Standards in Scottish Primary Schools'. The more specific ones are themselves interesting: 'Areas still using attainments tests at the transfer stage show gains about twice as large as those in other areas. . . . Little or no association was found between attainments in the Arithmetic tests and the use of Cuisenaire methods. . . . Higher attainments in the English tests go with greater provision of school libraries. . . . No association was found between attainments and the shortage of teachers'.

The committee were hesitant however to make the same kinds of comment on teaching that had been made ten years earlier. For the most part they simply drew attention to the items where there had been changes and those where there had not. Teachers and administrators are left free to draw their own conclusions. There is, however, the occasional reiteration of an earlier point: 'When one considers the extent to which Scots of some kind is spoken and understood, one can only conclude that Scots in print is completely unfamiliar to three quarters of the pupils of this age group. It would appear desirable to include some printed Scots among the reading material, for Scottish children'.

The national survey is, then, a familiar exercise in Scotland and we are able to judge its merits and benefits empirically in a way which is difficult in some other countries.

There have been larger scale surveys particularly in the United States where the National Assessment of Educational Progress (NAEP) programme is by far the largest yet undertaken. That survey involved four samples, 9, 13, 17 year olds and 'young adults', drawn to represent each state of the union. From the initial concentration on three subject areas—writing, science and citizenship—there has been expansion into reading, literature, mathematics, social sciences, career and occupational development, music and arts, each to be tested in a cycle that would involve no more than two or three subjects areas being involved in any one year of the programme. There was much more thought given to the contents of the test than in Scotland; or, at least, more of the effort put into deciding the content of the tests was recorded. Objectives are defined which have to be acceptable to subject specialists, teachers and 'thoughtful adults'. The items were chosen not to spread those taking the examinations for selection purposes (that is, they were not norm referenced) but rather they were intended to indicate what proportion of the age group had mastered a particular aspect of the subject (that is, they are criterion referenced). As with all criterion referencing there is a problem of validity and in this case content validity is determined by a lengthy process of review involving the three groups of specialists referred to above. The national assessment results indicate the proportion of the age group reaching the pre-defined criteria. These results are reported at length in bulletins which are prepared by NAEP and which attempt to interpret the meaning of the test results and not simply to report them.

In addition to the national survey a number of American States have initiated their own programmes. Perhaps the best known is the Michigan Educational Assessment

Programme which attempts to measure minimal performance objectives in the basic skill areas. These tests have been administered to fourth and seventh grade pupils. This programme has been subjected to considerable criticism, much of it arising from the publication of the scores for individual schools when the teachers concerned had been previously assured that the results would remain confidential. The criticism focused on the notion of minimal competence, pointing out that it was difficult to define and in any case was potentially stifling to all but the least able. There is also, as was pointed out in the first Scottish survey, a difficulty in interpreting scores on a criterion referenced test of this kind where schools have different curricular objectives.

In England and Wales the Assessment of Performance Unit (APU) has been established to carry out surveys of achievement there. Aware of some of the difficulties that have arisen in the United States and elsewhere, the APU has stressed that it is concerned with a cross curricular picture of national performance. That is, the achievement tests will be related not to specific curricula but to the general objectives of the curriculum. The areas to be the subject of tests are language, mathematics and science; three other areas, personal and social development aesthetic development and physical development are also being explored. The tests will be administered to national samples of 11, 13 and 15 year olds.

There have been national surveys in France of mother-tongue and mathematics; in Switzerland, of mathematics; and others, on a more limited scale, elsewhere. There is therefore sufficient experience both within Scotland and in other countries for it to be possible to look at the basic issues.

The first question we must ask is why should we monitor. The English APU answer that question in a general way in one of their leaflets; the purpose of monitoring, it says, is to provide national information 'not only to describe the current position but also to record changes as they occur' further, such information would both help determine national policy including decisions about the employment of resources and help teachers in planning the balance of pupils working in schools without an attempt at national level to define more detailed syllabus content. 'Moreover the outcome of the test will enable the APU to make parents, employers, and others concerned better informed about the achievement of schools.'

These statements beg a good few questions. Why do we want to describe the current position and to record changes as they occur? How will such information help to determine national policy? What help will be available to teachers for planning the balance of pupils work? Will test scores make parents, employers and others better informed about the achievements in schools? The first and fourth questions raised in the APU leaflet are the same. The fourth merely specifies a particular audience for information about the current position and any changes that might occur.

A major criticism of the American NAEP studies has been that they provided a lot of information but not much of it was useful. The most recent survey, for example, reported that only about one third of 17 year old students and more than half of adults knew that of four specified common household substances, salt is the best for putting out a grease fire. It is not at all clear what is to be done about that piece of information nor indeed who is to do it. What implications are there for national policy or for the balance of pupils work except the most trivial?

There are two sets of questions, one general and national, the other local and specific. It is doubtful whether a single set of tests could provide information relevant to both sets of issues. Information about the current position and/or changes is a recurring concern of those involved in the administration of education, of educational researchers and occasionally of those with a more general interest in the schools such as employers and academics. There are occasional flurries of interest in the national standards with headlines in the national press but they are usually followed by a period of quiescence. The 'Why Johnnie Can't Read' uproar in the United States and the Admiral Rickover complaints were followed by a period of apparent lack of interest in the whole issue. The efforts of the researchers to produce data, for example, the IEA studies, played very little part in the debate. Evidence seems to make little contribution in this particular discussion. It seems to deteriorate into the pub arguments of my youth which consisted of repetitions of 'Aye it is', 'Nay its not', repeated in gradually rising tones until the barman ejected the disputants.

The call for information about contemporary standards sounds reasonable enough but it is not at all clear what use would be made either of general information about the present or about comparisons with the past. There is, for example, considerable American evidence that the standards of candidates for the college entrance examination have been dropping steadily in recent years, but, since nobody knows why, there is not much that can be done about it. Similarly, if a national survey of primary schools standards were to indicate that very few 13 year olds could obtain a cube root without using a calculator, what would we do about it? What use would it be to know what the standards of attainment are nationally? Perhaps working parties could be established, memoranda issued and new curricula prepared, but would it be right to do so? Is the full apparatus of a national survey, definition of objectives, sampling frame and all, helpful for this purpose?

Similarly, recording changes as they occur is less obviously compelling on analysis. It seems self evident that we should monitor standards over time as a sort of quality control but what use can be made of the general information? When 'Rising Standards in Scottish Primary Schools' was published 10 years ago it was not exactly a best seller. No one seemed to want to know. Perhaps the problem lay in the title. Would a book entitled 'What has happened to standards in Scottish Primary Schools?' have sold better? Similarly the evidence that reading standards have not shifted, produced from renorming the Graded Work Reading Test, does not provide much of a basis as guide to national policy on staffing standards. If information is indeed to help national policy it must be designed to provide information about particular policy issues. It has been a wide-spread and legitimate criticism of national assessment that information provided is likely to relate to neither national issues nor to local.

It is arguable that what parents and employers and others need is not more information of a general kind about standards, but a better understanding of what it is that schools are setting out to achieve and how particular activities fit into these objectives. Employers need to know as a basis for discussion with educational authorities what arithmetic the schools are trying to teach and what communication skills are being taught. Parents need to know that apparently random play activities in Primary One or field studies in Secondary Four are carefully thought-out parts of an overall programme making a specified contribution to the childrens learning.

8

They also need to be reassured that the schools their own children attend are providing the same opportunity as are available to others. Surveys of national standards will not inform them on either of these points.

It is not only the general level of information which may be irrelevant to the real concerns of those involved in education but also the specific information. Why do we teach children arithmetic or reading? What effects do we expect it to have on them as adults? Are we moving to a society where the standards required of a minority will be far in excess of what we conventionally define as literacy or numeracy—and relate to an ability to absorb complex ideas presented in a variety of media and an ability to think mathematically about a range of problems—and for the majority be limited to the ability to find page 3 of the Daily Record and to do some very limited counting.

The appropriate standards required in a future society have to be defined and this is not an issue that can be burked by taking refuge in the use of established tests. The same applies to science and social studies. Do we merely wish children to be able to reproduce a series of facts, formulae and theories or to understand and use the scientific method? Is there a purpose to teaching about the Battle of Bannock-burn, and, if so, what is it and how could it be most effectively achieved?

The 'how' and the 'what' of educational assessment are manifestly dependant on the asking of *why*. What information we want to gain and how we will set about gaining it will depend on the use to which we wish to put it. It is clear that for the most part there will be a limited amount of formal information available from tests which are not based on the definition of 'detailed syllabus content', and which are not likely therefore to be closely correlated with activities within individual schools but dependant on the general opportunity to acquire information and skills provided by the culture and on the support provided by a particular social context. If what we want to do is to help determine national policy or help in planning the balance of pupils' work, then the information provided must relate closely to the issues of national policy or to the balance of pupils' work. In both cases there is a very close relationship to specific curricular issues and specific curricular procedures. It is instructive to refer back to the findings of the two Scottish surveys. A number of general conclusions were drawn from these studies. What impact did they have on policy? Some of the findings were negative but reassuring as differences among the four types of areas (cities, large towns, small towns and other areas) were small and not important. Differences in achievement of pupils from various geographical regions were small and not important. Pupils from smaller schools obtained practically the same standard as those in large schools. The pupils from one teacher schools reached the same standards as those obtained by pupils in schools with more than six teachers. That conclusion does not seem to have affected the policy of closing small schools. Are we to retain or return to attainment tests at the transfer stage because they seem to be related to higher standards on tests of the kind used in the surveys? Do we dismiss using Cuisenaire rods on the evidence of the survey? How many more primary schools libraries have been established because of the evidence of the survey? What implications are there for policy from the findings on the impact of the supply of teachers? Where there is significant evidence it has been largely overwhelmed by other considerations of the type referred to above. A notion of what primary education is meant to achieve is not adequately measured by formal tests, so that any advantage accruing to schools from use by the authority of attainment tests at the transfer stage may well be outweighed by other more negative effects on the curriculum of schools. And what about the teaching of Scots?

As the authors of the 1953 report wisely point out 'survey data throw no light on the important issue of class size. It seems clear that any investigation of this problem must not accept the given structure of classes with size already determined by administrative needs but must be specifically designed to test the effect of varying the size of class'. This is a conclusion which has relevance to the findings of the later studies. It might well be applied to cuisenaire rods, school libraries and teacher supply. Indirect evidence from surveys is partial, and evidence on these and many other issues is best obtained from experimental studies.

What contribution can surveys make to the work of teachers? The concern of teachers is rarely about standards as a whole. They have two interests. The first is in the standards of their own pupils compared with those in other similar schools. As with wages our reference groups tend to be local and individual rather than national and general. It is the question of each teacher defining for himself what standards are appropriate in his circumstances, finding out whether his pupils are reaching these standards and taking the appropriate action. The teacher's other interests is what he should teach and how he should teach it. National surveys cannot help any individual teacher to decide what teaching schemes should be used next year nor how it should be used and still less on the balance of work for particular pupils.

The specific advice to teachers in the scholastic surveys illustrates these limitations. Did many schools cease division by factors or pay more attention to the lay-out of short division sums or provide persistent oral practice in accepted speech forms? If they did, how many teachers would now think that was good advice? As with the more general issues the specific recommendations relate to a particular perception of the purposes of schools which is not now so widely held. Even for those who do accept the assumptions of the authors, how would a particular teacher know whether the more attention which, it is held, should be paid nationally to the lay-out of short division sums applied to his class? If he was already providing more attention than the average should he provide not more but perhaps less? Is it likely that those already giving considerable attention to the lay-out of short division sums would feel strengthened in their conviction and provide even more? Would those not giving sufficient attention have overlooked this point in the recommendations of the report? Findings from national survey may or may not apply to any particular teacher, and whether any teachers will take account of them will depend very much on their own values and their own perception of their current practice.

Those recommendations which are general are trivial and certainly do not require a national survey to justify them. In the case of the standardised notation for recording time of day, the survey merely indicated variation in practice. The panel's choice of a particular form arose not from the survey but from their own general experiences. Information which would be relevant to specific questions cannot for the most part be satisfactorily obtained from national surveys.

A teacher's decision about the emphasis to be given to science or social studies, reading or arithmetic is much more likely to be based on his own experience of the situation around him than on any information that the nation as a whole did well or badly in tests of science or social studies or in physics as compared with chemistry, or geography as compared with history. Individual teaching decisions are not made on this basis but on the basis of specific information which relates to the teacher's own objectives and the circumstances in which he is operating.

There are circumstances when national surveys can be useful for national policy making. These are mainly when the national conscience is agitated by specific educational issues. If there is concern about standards then national surveys may play some useful role in providing empirical evidence. Even then, as an article in the Consultative Committee on the Curriculum (CCC) News No. 2 demonstrates, there may be a tendency among the protagonists on one side or the other to question the survey evidence. Surveys may also have a publicity value in the same circumstances. The publicity given to a series of surveys of reading standards contributed to the atmosphere which made the establishment of the Bullock Committee acceptable. General surveys speak only to general issues. When information is required on other matters organisational or curricular then other, experimental, approaches are appropriate. What can and should be assessed provides considerable problems. In the preparation of any survey there are four decisions to be made. The first is the general area in which the testing is to be conducted. For example is this to be in the traditional subject matter areas or in applied skills? The second is the domains which are to be sampled. These domains are classes of objectives rather than specifically defined units of knowledge or skill. For example, in arithmetic, the ability to add all sets of two digit numbers could be a domain; in geography the domain might be the concept of pollution. The third step is the definition of the level at which the pupils are expected to function within the domain. Here taxonomies are helpful. Finally there is the definition of the standard. There must be a standard of achievement which is defined as satisfactory. There may of course be several standards for any given groups of pupils. There are also a number of sets of questions about the format of the tests, but these are quite separate and independent of these basic issues. The first task is to define the aspects of school work which are to be assessed. At the primary level, should assessments be related to the traditional divisions of arithmetic and English as in the Council's primary surveys of 25 years ago, or should they be inter-disciplinary and focused on the childrens' ability to solve particular problems, drawing on all the experiences the school provides? At the secondary level, can we accept the division into language, mathematics, science and social studies, or are these divisions artificial and should we concentrate on inter-disciplinary activities? Do we want to know whether a pupil has acquired the basic skills which would allow him to tackle particular problems or do we want to know whether he has also learned to apply the skills in a realistic situation? At its most fundamental level there may be a sharp distinction between the words a child can decipher, those which he can interpret and those which he can use. Similarly, in arithmetic there may be a gap between a pupil's ability to recite number facts and his ability to use his understanding of those numerical relationships. Whether the decision made is to follow the traditional curriculum structure or not (and in all major surveys this approach has been accepted), there is the problem of the specification of the content or domain to be tested. A domain refers to a class of measurable objectives rather than to a specific skill or area of knowledge. When a domain or class of objectives is defined it will usually be necessary to sample. In the example given above for geography, the class of objectives refers to those associated with an understanding of pollution. These could be sub-divided into air pollution, pollution of water, and so on. If in simple arithmetic the domain was addition of two digit numbers, there would have to be a selection of all possible combinations rather than an attempt to test them all. One technique which is helpful in clarifying thinking about the domain is the technique of facet analysis, which helps to ensure that there is a comprehensive coverage of all the different aspects of the subject being surveyed.

In the United States the NAEP has, as described above, used a series of successive sieves to select the material to be included in the tests. A series of reference groups, teachers curriculum specialists and parents and so on defined the objectives of instruction within particular subject areas. One might hear an echo of the Deweyite consensual or democratic definition of truth in this approach.

The APU has opted for a category system which is based on a rational analysis of the subject and which combines the two issues of domains and level. The categories are derived from three main criteria the structure of ideas of the subject, current issues and the psychological structure of the subject. The content or domains which emerge from this analysis at the primary level are measures in mathematics, geometry, number, algebra, probability and statistics. Each of these content areas or domains is related to the activity or level. A number of procedures have been devised to classify test items according to conceptual level. Perhaps the most familiar is Bloom *et al.*'s (1956) *Taxonomy of Educational Objectives* which refers to the cognitive area. The lowest level of this taxonomy is knowledge and at the higher levels analysis, synthesis and evaluation. Krathwohl *et al.*'s (1964) taxonomy refers to the affective area. Here the lowest level is attending and the highest characterisation. Simpson's (1966) classification of educational objectives with psychomotor area runs from perception to complex overt response. Another approach is Gagné's (1971) six category system which begins with reinstating and runs through to generating. Each of these approaches begins with recognition and recall and runs at the higher levels to generalisation and the application of concepts or theories. It has in the past been easier to get agreement about the more basic levels and test them than it has been to define and find acceptable measures of the more complex.

Finally, there is the need to define satisfactory criteria for levels of achievement. A national survey cannot place individuals on a scale though it could place groups, as in the case of the Scottish scholastic surveys, which asked whether pupils from different kinds of areas, from different geographical regions, from different kinds of schools fell into any specific order. Usually though, the intent is to provide indications about standards in some general or abstract sense. For this purpose tests like the NAEP tests which are criterion referenced are necessary. Defining the criteria in a general or abstract way may not be too difficult. In some fields it is possible to define them quite specifically and to measure them reliably. It is, for example, possible to see what proportion of ten year olds can swim 100 metres, 200 metres, 300 metres and so on. The criterion of being able to swim a given number of metres is reasonably specific and the individual behaviour is reasonably consistent. It is not as easy to define ability in reading as it is in swimming. Even at the simplest level of being able to give a sound value to visual cues, that is, to pronounce out loud written words, there are problems in defining the difficulty of words. Number of letters or number of syllabuses in a word, for example, are not necessary indicators of the difficulties. Familiarity may be more important. Even when the criteria are established there may well be hundreds of words falling into a particular category. Only some of them can be included in any particular assessment. A child is bound to make some errors. At what point do we say a child can recognise two letter words?

When he makes only one error out of ten words randomly selected from all two letter words? Or will we accept two errors or three or four?

The final question is 'how'. We now have sufficient experience of sampling procedures for a variety of purposes, particularly social science research, such that once the population has been defined it is relatively simple to provide a sampling procedure which will give results sufficiently close to the testing of the whole population to be acceptable. The advantages of sampling are two-fold. The first obvious one is the economy involved in sampling a small proportion of the total group, and the second, the ease of obtaining a sample where it might be difficult to reach all members of a population. The simplest approach is to draw a sample at random so that every member of the population has an equal chance of being selected. With a small population this is a feasible procedure. With a large population it is considerably more difficult so that a stratified sample is most often used. The population is classified into strata which are thought to be associated with the variable to be measured. In the sholastic survey, size of school was one and type of area was another. Schools were drawn from each category in proportion to the number in that category, thus a small proportion of the total population can be selected which can be expected to give results nearly identical with those likely to be obtained from the population as a whole.

A second dimension is added by matrix sampling. Not only is the population of children to be tested sampled but so is the population of items. In this way only a sample of items is administered to each individual in the sample of pupils. A relatively small demand is made upon the time of any individual yet information can be gathered on a wide range of items. If there are 20 or more categories of items each of which will have to include an adequate number of individual items for the score to be reliable, the total test might be overwhelming if administered in total to individual pupils. When the population of items as well as the population of pupils is sampled only a light sample is necessary and the demand made is acceptable.

Each of the three questions, 'why', 'what' and 'how' raises problems. The technical problems have received much attention since the first scholastic survey 25 years ago and acceptable solutions have been found to many of them. The other issues, what and why raise largely problems of value. They must be answered on other than research grounds. A decision has to be made about what should be assessed and that decision has to be reconciled with what can be assessed. A clear decision has to be made about the objectives of a survey and measures and techniques used which will meet those objectives. It is this reconciliation of means and ends that poses the most serious challenge for the national survey.

Bibliography

Assessment of Performance Unit. *Monitoring Mathematics.* DES, 1978.

Assessment of Performance Unit. *Why, What and How.* DES Information Division, 1977.

Bloom, B. S. *et al. Taxonomy of Educational Objectives Handbook: Cognitive Domain.* David McKay, 1956.

Gagné, R. M. *Defining Objectives for Six Types of Learning.* American Educational Research Association (Training Tape Series B Audiotape), 1971.

Krahtwohl, D. R. *et al. Taxonomy of Educational Objectives: Handbook II Affective Domain.* David McKay, 1964.

SCRE. *The Scottish Scholastic Survey,* 1953. University of London Press, 1963.

SCRE. *Rising Standards in Scottish Primary Schools.* University of London Press, 1968.

Sumner, R. (Ed.). *Monitoring National Standards of Attainment in Schools.* NFER, 1977.

ATTITUDE ASSESSMENT

In the later years of the 60's it was often said that the decade had been one in which concern had been for cognitive development and that the 70's would see the emergence of the affective domain as the dominant concern. In the last year of this decade it is probably safe to say that the prediction has not come true. That there has been concern, there is no doubt, but the concern has been more about 'whether' than 'when', 'what' and 'how'. Attitudinal objectives are stated for many new courses of instruction. Sometimes teaching strategies and methods are suggested which should lead to the establishing of such attitudes. Seldom are methods for assessing their achievement suggested and even less seldom are they assessed.

Many teachers are wary of venturing into this field, some because of the difficulties they see in finding suitable teaching techniques, others because they believe that they will in some way be infringing their pupils' privacy, and suitable methods available or not, they are not morally justified in attempting to deal with such objectives. The Assessment of Performance Unit of the DES has set up an exploratory group to consider whether it would be possible to monitor the personal and social development of English pupils. Although it has not begun to discuss whether to monitor or not, the National Union of Teachers has publicly stated its opposition to any examination of such matters.

Dr Sally Brown, Senior Research Fellow in the Education Department of Stirling University has been involved in the assessment of attitudes for some years now. She undertook an evaluation of the achievement of the affective objectives in the Integrated Science Curriculum in Scotland and, among other things, developed instruments for assessing the extent to which the attitudes desired by the curriculum authors were actually held by the pupils following the course. This review of the present position is therefore well founded on experience in the field and should prove useful in the continuing debate at all levels in the education system concerning the attitudes of pupils at all stages. The report 'Pupils in Profile' wants attitudes assessed, the Dunning Report wants attitudes assessed, many headteachers in primary and secondary schools are asking their teachers to provide views on pupils' attitudes. Can they be assessed? Further, once assessed how precise, how permanent are any results obtained? Are we indeed infringing privacy and therefore have no business to attempt such assessment? These are some of the questions to which we must all find answers before too long.

A.W.J.

15

Attitude Assessment

Sally Brown

The Nature of Attitude Objectives

Over the last fifteen years considerable emphasis has been placed on the attitudes that pupils develop through the instruction they receive. This has been reflected in the attitude objectives of the new curricula, and these objectives can be seen to be of a number of different kinds. Some relate solely to feelings or emotions (*e.g.* 'enjoyment') that pupils may experience in the classroom, and may be described as purely *affective* in nature. Others are concerned with *awareness;* they seem to have little to do with pupils' feelings but relate to rather ill-defined cognitive behaviours (*e.g.* 'recognises that the primary activity in science is study of the natural world'). A third group are directed towards the development of *values* (*e.g.* 'The student will view problems in objective, realistic and tolerant terms'). Values may be seen as enduring beliefs that particular ways of going about things are preferable to the alternatives (Rokeach, 1973); they provide standards and motivation for personal conduct, have an affective component (one feels good or bad about it), tend to be deep rooted and 'all' or 'nothing' in nature, and are probably difficult to change. The fourth group, which may be seen as genuine *attitude* objectives, differ from values in that they are directed towards specific objects or phenomena (*e.g.* 'Pupils should develop negative attitudes towards smoking'), they may be positive or negative and may vary in degree. There is little consensus on a definition of 'attitude' but it is convenient to view each one as having an affective component (*e.g.* 'Pupils feel negatively about smoking'), a cognitive component (*e.g.* 'Pupils have bits of knowledge about the ill-effects of smoking') and a tendency to act in a particular way (*e.g.* 'Pupils avoid establishing a habit of smoking').

It appears, then, that objectives labelled as 'attitudes' cover a range of characteristics that are well described by Alpren's (1973) definition of education in the affective domain:

> '*Provision for the growth of attitudes and behaviours that deal with feelings, values and, in general, the personal concerns of students*'.

As Alpren suggests, this covers a wide range of issues from 'the province of psycho-analysis' to such things as the 'aim of helping students to "appreciate mathematics"'. This paper is concerned with issues exemplified by the latter rather than the former, and 'attitudes' will be taken as covering the range of meaning implied by the different curriculum objectives described above rather than in the narrower psychological sense.

Responsibility for Attitudes in Teaching

Curricula and tests in Scotland have traditionally concentrated on cognitive achievement. However, concern with pupils' low motivation, poor attitudes towards school and subjects and inadequate appreciation of environmental/societal issues among the general population is focusing attention on the affective domain. Some of the concern is for long-term goals that relate not so much to what pupils will be able to do after instruction as to what they will choose to do. In other words, the teaching is to be directed towards ensuring that pupils' *typical behaviour* will conform to certain desirable criteria and the development of particular attitudes and values is no longer to be left to chance.

A second type of concern is for affective goals that relate to *motivation*. The concept of mastery learning presents one of the more coherent forms of the argument in this area: pupils' attitudes to school, subjects and themselves are crucial to success in learning; success in learning is a determinant of the affective outcomes of any task; and those affective outcomes will be reflected in the zeal, curiosity and interest with which the next task is approached. Klopfer (1971) asserts that 'There is strong psychological evidence that students learn better, learn more and remember longer when they find pleasure in the learning experience'. Many would agree, but the empirical evidence for relationships between affective and cognitive variables among pupils is equivocal, (*cf.* Alvord, 1972 and Gardner, 1975, with Khan and Wiess, 1973) and suggests that these relationships are complex.

Similar affective goals, that look like aspects of motivation, are justified as feelings and experiences that have *inherent qualities;* thus enjoyment, interest and curiosity in classroom tasks and activities are seen as valuable in themselves and not as merely means to cognitive ends.

It may also be argued that even when a curriculum has no explicit attitude objectives there will always be *implicit affective goals:*

'most educators, at least when pressed, affirm the importance of enhancing curiosity and of implanting in the student massive and enduring positive affect towards learning and subject matter. Most of us would agree, therefore, that even when an instructional program does not attempt to enhance positive attitudes directly, these variables should be monitored if possible in the evaluation of the program to guard against unintended decreases in interest or involvement.' (Messick, 1970).

Enthusiastic promotion of affective goals is one thing, decisions on the nature (or even the occurrence) of assessment in the area of attitudes are another, and such decisions depend crucially on the morality and rationality of our acceptance of responsibility for this sort of pupil learning.

McIntyre (1977) has dealt very thoroughly with these issues. He points out that if teachers are to be responsible for moulding either pupils' temporary feelings (*e.g.* interest or curiosity during lessons), or their future affective characteristics, or behaviours (*e.g.* lasting interest in a subject or typical pattern of objectively assessing evidence presented), then inevitably pupils' autonomy will be infringed either temporarily during lessons or more permanently. A value judgement has, therefore, to be made about the relative importance of pupils' autonomy and of the acquisition of non-cognitive attributes that are seen as desirable.

In practice, curriculum developers frequently seem to want the best of both of these worlds. For example, Curriculum Paper 7 (Scottish Education Department, 1969) suggests that 'the attitudes which these young people form should be *their own decisions*, based on reasonably objective information' (my emphasis); yet if we look at such attitude objectives as that of pupils acquiring 'an interest in and a willingness to participate in the conservation of the natural environment' we find that in reality there is only one decision that the pupil is expected to come to. It seems likely that if all the 'reasonably objective information' available were to be considered, there would be many contexts in which the pupil would *not* be favourable to 'the conservation of the natural environment'.

The question of what we should ask teachers to accept responsibility for in the affective domain depends not only on what we judge they *ought* to do but also on what we rationally expect they *can* do. McIntyre (1977, pp. 24–26) provides a summary of a number of different kinds of evidence that indicate something of the nature and quality of the knowledge acquired by teachers through their own experience, about what effects their teaching has on pupils. Although he concludes from at least one study (Jackson, 1968) that teachers may be willing to accept responsibility for interest and enthusiasm among their pupils, he finds little to convince him that they are rationally justified in doing so. He points to evidence that teachers perceive pupils in highly global ways that are unlikely to provide accurate judgements of such things as pupils' interest (Hallworth, 1962; Morrison *et al.*, 1965) and to the fact that teachers' perceptions of pupils' satisfactions and interest relate much more closely to measures of IQ or cognitive attainment than they do to pupils' own assessments of satisfaction and interest (Jackson, 1978; Brown, 1975). He concludes 'if teachers' knowledge of pupils' thinking and feeling is as crude and inaccurate as such evidence suggests, it is difficult to imagine how they can make sensible decisions about how to influence pupils' experiences and mental activities'. Furthermore, he demonstrates that theoretical knowledge based on research has little more to offer teachers about how to make judgments about pupils' feelings, or how to decide on appropriate courses of action to influence them in desirable ways.

Even if we can hypothesise a situation where someone (pupil, teacher or curriculum developer) will be held accountable for affective learning, there is still the problem of whether we can assess that learning. If the concern is with pupils' feelings we have to remember that feelings are *mental* activities and can only be *inferred* from observable regularities of behaviour. We have to be confident that we understand how feelings are manifest in behaviour and that we are in a position to lead pupils to display that behaviour. Can we, for example, be sure we can both reliably recognise 'curiosity' in pupils' behaviours and persuade them to display those behaviours? Are we in a position to specify the behaviours that reflect values such as 'openmindedness', can we lead pupils to display them and will we have the opportunity to assess the endurance of such qualities?

However, we may be directly concerned with the behavioural component of attitudes rather than feelings: *feeling* motivated is no good if a pupil does not *act* motivated, and that action may be influenced by factors, unrelated to interest or feelings about the work, such as classroom conditions, peer responses, teachers' manipulations and the pupil's self-image. *Feelings* about taking up a career in X are irrelevant unless reflected in the *number and quality of candidates* making themselves available for such careers.

The Purposes of Attitude Assessment

In exploring the purposes of affective assessment the discussion will centre, firstly, on that relating to the *individual* pupil and, secondly, on that concerned with *groups* of pupils.

We may wish to *grade individual pupils for certification or selection purposes*. Arguments for this are sparse in the literature since there are both practical and moral stumbling blocks: firstly, criterion measures that would be needed to assess whether or not a pupil had, for example, attained a particular attitude are not readily available; and, secondly, many people are uneasy about the morality of, say, selecting pupils on the basis of how their attitudes rank with those of other pupils.

It is unusual to find such grading recommended for primary school pupils, but there are a number of examples of attitude measures being used or suggested for certification at the secondary level in the United Kingdom. The Headteachers' Association of Scotland (1977) defend their recommendation for assessment of non-cognitive characteristics in 'Pupil Profiles' as being what employers want and as 'justice especially to our less academic pupils. . . . They may rate highly for some behaviours—"Persistence", "Reliability"—while failing in written examinations.' However, the characteristics they choose to assess, 'Perseverance' and 'Enterprise', are not easily distinguishable in behavioural terms from cognitive abilities. Indeed, the evaluators of the profiles scheme appear to validate the characteristics in relation to abilities when they provide a 'ready explanation' for some teachers giving adverse assessments on 'Perseverance' and 'Enterprise' as 'the fact that less able pupils are commonly allocated to these courses'.

This scheme curiously neglects moral justifications for their use of non-cognitive assessments on a four point scale in a normative mode (despite teachers' preference for comments, and parental and teacher concern about the detrimental effect of low gradings on pupils' futures). After asserting that the assessments should be made and incorporated into a school leaving certificate, the authors state that they 'have not intended to place these behaviours on a moral scale. Adaptability is not necessarily a virtue. Willingness to co-operate may be a fault.' Do they imagine that a low grade in 'Perserverance' will impress a future employer?

On the practical side, the problems of ensuring that 'Perseverance' and 'Enterprise' are interpreted in the same way by different teachers, across different subjects and on different occasions, together with the difficulties of identifying behaviours that will validly reflect such characteristics of pupils, are side-stepped by giving no interpretation of the meaning of the terms, and by leaving the issue of how to make the assessment squarely in the teachers' hands. Unfortunately, the evidence suggests that under such conditions teachers' assessments of non-cognitive characteristics are subject to errors that 'are so serious that statements about pupils reveal more about the attitudes of the rater than they do about the pupil.' (Ingenkamp, 1976, p. 179).

It is encouraging to find that the Dunning Report (Scottish Education Department, 1977) on assessment in the third and fourth years of secondary education in Scotland expresses doubt (paragraph 4.11) about the inclusion of assessment of such non-cognitive characteristics on pupils' leaving certificates.

Mathews (1974) outlines the Nuffield 'A' Level Chemistry examination scheme where 3 per cent of the examination mark is based on teachers' assessment of attitudes to practical work, and the Schools' Council Integrated Science 'O' Level where 8 per cent of the mark relates to teachers' assessments of the achievement of a number of affective objectives. He welcomes these teacher-based measures and says:

'Provided that there are suitable safeguards to prevent injustice to individual candidates and for moderation between one teacher's marks and another's, there seems no reason why the first tentative steps in assessment should not be extended to other subjects'.

Despite the cautious nature of this statement, it is irresponsible in ignoring fundamental problems of this sort of measure. Firstly, the argument has been that such assessments cannot be made by an outside agency; they must be carried out by the teacher who has regular and continued contact with the pupil. Since another teacher would be an outside agency, what meaning does 'moderation between one teacher's marks and another's' have? Secondly, teachers' ratings of pupils' attitudes are notorious for the low correlations (Jackson, 1968; Brown, 1976) that exist between them and pupils' self-assessments of their own attitudes (and self-assessments are seen by Mathews as the most important source of information). Thirdly, teachers do not have the skills that enable them to validly identify behavioural indicators of attitudes; they need training and experience to carry out such tasks. Even when descriptions of behaviours relating to particular levels of development of various attitudes are provided, Harlen (1978) reports that those teachers not involved in the development and discussion of the behaviour lists 'failed to grasp the relevance to their teaching'.

Each of these three types of problem reflects some aspect of the validity of teachers' assessments of pupils. If such assessments are to be accepted, then it must be established that they accurately reflect those attributes of pupils that they purport to measure; and, at present, we have little reason to believe that they do.

If, instead of using teachers' ratings, pupils responses or self-assessments were accepted, other problems would arise. As Mathews (1974) points out:

'The assessment of attitudes depends very largely on the co-operation of the respondents and on honest replies from them; and if such assessments were to have any significant weight in selection procedures, or if pupils were to be subjected to penalties or criticism as a result of it, it is too much to expect that they would willingly give answers which would put them at a disadvantage.'

A second purpose of assessing individual's attitudes might be the *prediction of later achievement* and its use for curricular or vocational guidance. There is little doubt that counsellors and guidance teachers assess pupils on interests, preferences, and characteristics like self-reliance; those judgements may then be used to steer pupils towards particular careers or courses. However, relationships between non-cognitive characteristics and later achievements are by no means well established. Brown (1976), for example, reports that measures of five different attitudes to science among pupils on entry to Scottish secondary schools could account for not more than 7 per cent of the variation in science achievement among the pupils two years later.

Somewhat muted encouragement has been officially given (Scottish Education Department, 1977, paragraphs 2.5, 2.28 and 8.3) for the use for pupil guidance purposes of measures of affective characteristics such as those recommended by the Headteachers' Association of Scotland (1977). The dubious validity of teachers' ratings of these characteristics and the apparent failure of pupils' own responses to predict achievement suggests that such encouragement is premature.

Teachers' use of affective measures for *diagnosis, monitoring progress and guiding the learning* of pupils constitutes a third possible purpose for such assessment

(Mathews, 1974). If the intention is to help pupils then they may well be motivated to co-operate and to provide honest answers to questions. Mathews argues for frequent and rigorous assessment of pupils' attitudes to be incorporated into the design of new courses. The 'Progress in Learning Science' project (Harlen, Darwin and Murphy, 1977) is one of the few attempts that have been made to diagnose the stages of development of attitudes and 'match' activities to those stages. Despite great emphasis on teacher involvement in the work and on preparation of check-lists of behaviour for the diagnosis, there are still problems that relate to the management of such assessment in the classroom (Elliott, 1977), and the linkage between the diagnosis and choice of activity is relatively underdeveloped. Basically, we are still at a *research* stage and need to develop and test theories of relationships between the various elements of learning (characteristics of the individual, the environment, the social group and the instruction) in such a way that diagnosis of attitudes may be linked to appropriate treatment. However, it is worth pointing out that the most likely way that we can take valid and effective account of pupils' attitudes in the choice of activities for them is to let *them* choose among activities of which they have some experience. Such an assessment of short-term attitudes could be valid but would be superfluous since their attitudes would already have been taken account of in allowing them to choose.

If we turn now from assessment of the individual to that of the group, then we encounter one of the more plausible arguments for affective assessment: we have formulated objectives in the affective domain; therefore, it must be our intention that teachers teach towards such objectives. It is self-evident that we should assess pupils' feelings and affective attainment to see if the objectives have been achieved.

This argument may reflect concern with:

1. how effective a curriculum is in relation to its stated objectives or in comparison with some other curriculum;

2. how effective different teaching styles are in the affective domain;

3. how a teacher can judge whether he or she is doing a good job;

4. how teachers may be held accountable to the public for what they do and what they say they do.

All these concerns relate to the ways in which, and the extent to which, the affect of *groups* of pupils changes as a result of instruction. (Group measures will, however, normally be derived from assessments of individuals *e.g.* mean values of individual attitude scores may be used; or, a criterion may be that all or some proportion of the pupils exhibit specified attitude-related behaviours).

If interest centres on any of the first three concerns above, then the purpose of assessment of attitudes among the group will normally form part of a *curriculum evaluation, research or self evaluation study*. Such assessment may be very informative if two caveats are borne in mind:

1. If *understanding* of the instruction is sought, little progress will result from assessment of affective outcomes unless one starts with, or at an early stage works towards, a clear theoretical framework, *i.e.* the hypothesised 'means' for achieving the desired affective 'ends' should be demonstrably present in the

curriculum materials or in the specified characteristics of the teaching styles. There is little point in repeated testing for outcomes that are hoped for, but cannot rationally be expected;

2. There are problems in operationalising many of the affective objectives that are found in curricula. The difficulty appears to be twofold. Firstly, it is not clear what behaviours we should look for when we are concerned with such things as interests, attitudes and appreciations. Secondly, there is uncertainty about what are the phenomena related to education about which we expect pupils to display feelings or attitudes. A very interesting paper by Klopfer (1976) has gone a long way towards clarifying these issues in science education. He presents a grid in which one dimension consists of four categories of phenomena towards which some affective behaviour by the pupil is sought ('events in the natural world', 'activities', 'science' and 'enquiry'). The other dimension of the grid consists of five categories of affective pupil behaviours ('receiving', 'responding', 'valuing', 'organisation' and 'characterisation by a value') that are derived from the Taxonomy of Education Objectives—Affective Domain (Krathwohl, Bloom and Masia, 1964). Klopfer provides sample statements of objectives to illustrate the phenomena he includes and to indicate how the various behaviours impinge on these phenomena. The importance of this paper goes beyond science education: some of the phenomena are not science-specific while others may be readily adapted for other areas. The grid and examples form an excellent basis for clarifying objectives or developing items for assessment instruments, and the whole scheme provides a synoptic structure for the affective domain that enables us to move on from the position where we assert that attitudes are important in education but do not find it easy to say what that assertion means.

If the purpose of assessing the attitudes of groups of pupils relates to *teacher accountability*, then we have to be sure that we are justified in asking teachers to accept responsibility for pupils' affective experiences and learning. From the discussion of the previous section it appears we have little rational basis for holding teachers responsible for their pupils' temporary affective responses during instruction, none for asking them to accept responsibility for long term affective characteristics of pupils and sparse justification for using assessment of pupils' attitudes as an element in an accountability scheme.

Methods of Assessment

If useful purposes for attitude measurement in education can be identified, there are a variety of methods that may be used for such assessment. However, all of them have certain limitations.

It may be argued that what pupils are seen to be doing in classrooms is indicative of their attitudes and that teachers are in an excellent position to carry out *direct observation of such behaviour*. However, we have seen that teachers' ratings do not correlate well with pupils' self-assessments, and there is evidence that the ratings may be inappropriately inferring attitudes from academic performance. Even when appropriate behaviours are identified carefully, many teachers (and almost all outside agencies) do not have sufficient opportunities to observe their pupils and so make reliable assessments. There is also the difficulty that behaviour is not determined by a single attitude. It is influenced by the pupils' other attitudes, their expectations of peer response to their behaviour, constraints imposed on them by authority and their own intellectual, social or physical abilities. Clearly we have to be cautious in making decisions on the basis of teachers' direct observations of pupils' behaviour, but the salience of that behaviour among our concerns suggests that we should endeavour to develop valid and effective observation skills (at least for research purposes).

If pupils' self-assessments are sought, we may consider using a *direct question* to elicit a pupil's statement of his own attitude. There are, unfortunately, a number of problems with this approach: individuals may be reluctant to express their true feelings and may try to conform to what they believe the questioner wants (particularly if that is the teacher); answers to simple direct questions are easy to fake; pupils may not be aware of their own attitudes and so may not understand the question; and single questions may tap only one aspect of an attitude.

Collections of items in *attitude scales* are less open to faking and provide attitude 'scores' that have considerably higher validity and reliability than direct questions. In Thurstone scales, the items form a series of statements of different, measured intensities that reflect attitudes from the very favourable, through neutral to very unfavourable; pupils are asked to tick statements with which they agree. Ideally, only one item, indicating the intensity of that pupil's attitude, should be endorsed since statements above or below will correspond to attitudes of different intensities; in practice, where pupils' attitudes are not very clearly formed, this seldom happens. Guttman scales also have a series of items, but they are constructed in such a way that the ticking of any statement requires that all the statements of lower rank will be endorsed. Likert scales consist of items that reflect moderately favourable and moderately unfavourable attitudes; pupils indicate their own attitudes by indicating their agreement (or not) with each item on a 5 point scale. All these scales are easy to administer but their construction is time-consuming and complex (see Edwards, 1957 and Oppenheim, 1966). If appropriate and valid scales were constructed by experts and made available there is no reason why they should not be used by teachers for such things as comparisons among groups of pupils or the effects of curricular changes on the attitudes of groups; however, attitude scales are not suitable for ranking pupils or for gaining insights into the attitudes of individuals.

Attitude scales provide a closed structure within which pupils are expected to respond; a more open-ended means of obtaining information uses *essays* or *interviews* that focus on the attitude in question but do not restrict the pupils' responses in the same way. If such procedures are employed by teachers, Mathews (1974) observes 'The assessment could be strongly subjective and its validity and reliability in doubt'. Nevertheless, in experienced hands, content analyses of structured or semi-structured interviews can be very illuminating, and participant observation techniques that focus on informal interviews can provide valuable insights into the ways in which pupils construe, and have feelings about, their classroom experiences.

Open-ended procedures have been extended into *projective techniques* (Oppenheim, 1966) which set a variety of tasks for pupils (*e.g.* sentence completion, picture interpretation) for which the purpose is not obviously assessment of attitudes. On the assumption that there will be less opportunity for faking responses, clinical psychologists have used these techniques extensively to probe deeper levels of attitudes. Considerable skill and experience is needed for such work and while they may be valuable for individual cases, in group situations such tests are found wanting.

The *semantic differential* and *repertory-grid* techniques (Oppenheim, 1966) are useful for exploring the profiles and nature of individuals' attitudes towards various aspects of what they learn. While they are predominantly research instruments and require users to be adequately trained, they are flexible tools that allow the different sorts of feelings that pupils have towards subjects and instruction to be revealed together with the different ways in which an individual 'sees' the world of school and learning. These techniques may well be developed in the future in such a way that teachers may use them to gain insight into their pupils' attitudes. It seems unlikely, however, that such instruments could be used in ways that would relate directly to attitude objectives of the sort that have been discussed.

Instruments for assessment of values of the kind reflected in curriculum objectives are not readily available. The few value scales that are widely used (*e.g.* Allport, Vernon and Lindzey, 1951) have little direct relevance for educational issues.

This discussion has concentrated on assessment of affective characteristics; attitudes clearly have cognitive features. For example, it is unlikely that pupils will develop attitudes favourable to dental care unless they understand that it will contribute in some way to their well-being. Just how attitudes and knowledge interact is a complex question and the focus of numerous psychological theories, but there is general agreement that where peoples' attitudes towards something are inconsistent with their knowledge about that thing, the situation will be one of discomfort and the attitudes will be likely to change. This will not be the case if coercion is being used to change attitudes; in that event the initial attitudes may be reinforced.

This attitude-knowledge interdependence is recognised in the 'awareness' objectives of curricula; for example, desirable attitudes towards community health may be seen as depending on pupils becoming 'aware of their potential to improve current health standards' (SED, 1974). Such 'awareness' can be tested by cognitive tests of attainment but may or may not indicate underlying attitudes. The knowledge may well be supportive to formation of the attitude, but acquisition of information (particularly under coercion) can lead to very negative attitudes on the part of pupils; Eiss and Harbeck (1969) list ten factors that often cause pupils to lose interest in science and nine of these are concerned with pupils' cognitive learning. The evidence that is available from studies of classrooms that have looked at pupils' attitudes to classroom work or subjects suggests that the teaching which tends to promote positive attitudes tends not to be closely related to that promoting high attainment (*e.g.* Dunkin and Biddle, 1974). There is evidence of a trend for courses in such things as environmental health, safety and social education to be as concerned about attitudes and values as about knowledge: *e.g.*

'The aim should be to ensure that all young people approach the responsibilities of growing up in an enlightened and sensitive way, with knowledge of their physical nature and an appreciation of the moral and spiritual factors involved in their relationship with another person'.

(Scottish Education Department, 1974)

We are probably in a position to assess achievement of the knowledge aim but we do not have the means for assessing a pupil's endurable set of values; the most we might be able to do is to assess some of the related attitudes.

Summary

This paper has outlined the range of meanings that are attached to attitude goals, and has pointed to some difficult moral judgements to be made and practical issues to be dealt with if we are to apportion responsibility to the teacher (or anyone else) for pupils' attitude development. These are issues which have to be resolved if we are to justify the various purposes we may have for assessment of the attitudes of individual, or groups of, pupils.

The discussion of these various purposes has suggested: that where the concern is for certification or selection of individuals, the moral justifications and practical problems of making valid attitude assessments have been neglected; that assessment of attitudes for prediction of later achievement has been recommended for use for guidance purposes regardless of the poor predictive validity that current measures of attitudes display; that curriculum evaluation and research provide potentially fruitful areas for attitude assessment though efforts are needed to clarify the meanings of affective goals; and that there is little basis, either moral or rational, for assessment of pupils' attitudes as an element of teacher accountability schemes.

A variety of methods for attitude assessment have been reviewed; most require substantial adaptation for use for educational purposes and many require skills and training that teachers cannot normally be expected to have; some of the assessment related to attitudes seems to be of a cognitive nature, but the relationships between cognitive learning and development of attitudes in the classroom are complex and little understood.

Assessment of attitudes in education is at a primitive stage, partly because of confusion about the meanings of terms (*e.g.* 'attitude', 'appreciation') and inadequacy of assessment instruments (Krathwohl and Payne, 1971). But, more fundamentally, the purposes of, and justifications for, teaching towards attitude goals and assessing their achievement have not been given close enough scrutiny; and that scrutiny involves examination of the moral and rational basis of the demands that are made upon teachers or pupils in asking them to accept responsibilities in the affective domain.

References

Allport, G. W., Vernon, P. G. and Lindzey, G. (1951). *Study of Values*. Boston: Houghton-Mifflin.

Alpren, M. (1973). *Curriculum Significance of the Affective Domain*. Paper presented to Professors of Curriculum Annual Meeting, Minneapolis, March, 1973. ED 087 666.

Alvord, D. J. (1972). 'Achievement and attitude'. *The Science Teacher*, 39(4), 36–38.

Brown, S. A. (1975). *Affective Objectives in an Integrated Science Curriculum*. Unpublished Ph.D. thesis, University of Stirling.

Brown, S. A. (1976). *Attitude Goals in Secondary School Science*. Stirling Educational Monographs No. 1, University of Stirling: Department of Education.

Dunkin, M. J. and Biddle, B. J. (1974). *The Study of Teaching*. New York: Holt, Rinehart and Winston.

Edwards, A. L. (1957). *Techniques of Attitude Scale Construction*. New York: Appleton-Century-Crofts, Inc.

Eiss, A. F. and Harbeck, M. B. (1969). *Behavioural Objectives in the Affective Domain*. Washington D.C.: National Science Supervisors' Association.

Elliott, J. (1977). *Some Key Concepts Underlying Teachers' Evaluations of Innovation*. Paper presented to the British Educational Research Association Conference, University of Nottingham, September, 1977.

Gardner, P. L. (1975). 'Attitudes to science: a review'. *Studies in Science Education*, 2, 1–42.

Hallworth, H. J. (1962). 'A teacher's perception of his pupils'. *Educational Review*, 14, 124–133.

Harlen, W. (1978). *Implementation Through Involvement in Development Processes*. Paper presented to Bat-Sheva Seminar on Curriculum Implementation, Jerusalem, Israel, August, 1978.

Harlen, W., Darwin, A. and Murphy, M. (1977). *Match and Mismatch: Raising Questions; Leader's Guide; Finding Answers*. Edinburgh: Oliver and Boyd.

Headteachers' Association of Scotland (1977). *Pupils in Profile*. London: Hodder and Stoughton.

Ingenkamp, K. (1976). *Educational Assessment*. London: NFER Publishing Company.

Jackson, P. W. (1968). *Life in Classrooms*. New York: Holt, Rinehart and Winston.

Khan, S. B. and Weiss, J. (1973). 'The teaching of affective responses' in *Second Handbook of Research on Teaching*. Travers, R. (Ed.) pp. 759–804. New York: Rand McNally.

Klopfer, L. E. (1971). 'Evaluation of learning in science' in *Handbook of Formative and Summative Evaluation of Student Learning*. pp. 559–641. London: McGraw-Hill Book Company.

Klopfer, L. E. (1976). 'A structure for the affective domain in relation to science education'. *Science Education*, 60(3), 299–312.

Krathwohl, D. R., Bloom, B. S. and Masia, B. B. (1964). *Taxonomy of Educational Objectives Handbook 2: Affective Domain*. London: Longmans.

Krathwohl, D. R. and Payne, D. A. (1971). 'Defining and assessing educational objectives' in *Educational Measurement* (second edition), Thorndike, R. L. (Ed.) pp. 17–45. Washington: American Council on Education.

McIntyre, D. I. (1977). *What Responsibilities Should Teachers Accept?*. Stirling Educational Seminar Papers No. 1, University of Stirling: Department of Education.

Mathews, J. C. (1974). 'The assessment of attitudes' in *Techniques and Problems of Assessment*, pp. 172–185. Macintosh, H. G. (Ed.). London: Arnold.

Messick, S. (1970). 'The criterion problem in the evaluation of instruction: assessing possible, not just intended outcomes' in *The Evaluation of Instruction: Issues and Problems*, Wittrock, M. C. and Wiley, D. E. (Eds.), pp. 183–202. New York: Holt, Rinehart and Winston.

Morrison, A., McIntyre, D. and Sutherland, J. (1965). 'Teachers' personality ratings of pupils in Scottish primary schools'. *British Journal of Educational Psychology*, 35.

Oppenheim, A. N. (1966). *Questionnaire Design and Attitude Measurement*. London: Heinemann Educational Books.

Rokeach, M. (1973). *The Nature of Human Values*. New York: Free Press.

Scottish Education Department (1969). *Curriculum Paper 7: Science for General Education*. Edinburgh: HMSO.

Scottish Education Department (1974). *Curriculum Paper 14: Health Education in Schools.* Edinburgh: HMSO.

Scottish Education Department (1977). *Assessment for All.* Edinburgh: HMSO.

Acknowledgements

I would like to express my gratitude to the *Scottish Education Department* for providing the grant for my work, of which this paper is a part, and to *Donald McIntyre* for helpful and constructive criticism.

NORM-REFERENCED AND CRITERION-REFERENCED TESTS—AN EVALUATION

Dr Albert Pilliner was, until his recent retiral, Director of the Godfrey Thomson Unit for Academic Assessment in the University of Edinburgh and, as such, has been concerned about criterion and domain-referenced testing since its inception. In this paper he not only provides a brief and very readable description of the form and function of such tests but charts very clearly the differences between such tests and the more commonly encountered norm-referenced test.

The paper also makes clear that many of the difficulties involved in this new form of testing have not yet been resolved to everyone's satisfaction. Dr Pilliner, for example, indicates the complexity of determining the universe of items necessary to test so simple a thing as the addition of two numbers, 81 items being required, since not all are equally difficult for the student to solve and it would be unreasonable to subject him or her to all 81. The further problem then arises of how to obtain an acceptable representative sample. What manner of difficulty will arise when it is the 16-year-old student's ability to master the writing of an application for a job which has to be tested, or the 13-year-old's skills in solving scientific problems? The question we must all ask ourselves is which areas of the curriculum are—and which are not—susceptible to this form of testing. A further problem not covered in the paper but of considerable importance to any post Munn/Dunning considerations has recently been posed, that of mastery learning.

The Dunning Report has recommended the use of criterion-referenced tests particularly for Foundation level work, and there is no doubt that such procedures have much to commend them. Yet this form of testing is associated with a particular form of teaching strategy not often practised in Scottish schools, that of mastery learning. Dettrick* (1977) has recently argued that norm-referenced testing is associated with a classification system of education while criterion-referenced testing is associated with mastery techniques and that it is not possible to use properly the one form of testing on the unassociated system of education. If we continue to classify our potential Credit and General students, will it be possible to run both systems in a school at the same time? This paper should be read in the light of these latter observations.

A.W.J.

---

*Dettrick, G. W. *Models of Schooling & Models of Evaluation.* Paper presented at Annual Conference of Australian Association for Research in Education. Canberra, 1977.

Norm-Referenced and Criterion-Referenced Tests—An Evaluation

A. E. G. Pilliner

Q: Are norm-referenced tests different from criterion-referenced tests?

A: Yes, and speaking for both sides, *vive la différence*.

Hieronymus, A. N. 'Today's Testing' (page 66). In 'Educational Change: Implications for Measurement'. Proceedings of the 1971 Invitational Conference on Testing Problems. Princeton, Educational Testing Service, 1971.

Measurement—the need for a reference frame

When we measure, we do so in order to obtain information useful in some way. A police official measures the height of a young man seeking to enter the police force in order to determine whether he is above the minimum height prescribed in police regulations. A doctor measures the weight, or change in weight, of a patient in order to help diagnose his illness. A navigator on an airliner measures its airspeed in order to estimate the time of arrival. An educationist or psychologist uses tests of various kinds to measure aspects of human behaviour in order to provide information which will help him make intelligent decisions about people leading to appropriate action.

All these instances of measurement have two things in common. First, an instrument of some kind is used in each—a ruler, a weighing-machine, an airspeed indicator, a test or examination. Second, all that these instruments provide is information, of no interest in itself but an essential ingredient in a decision-making process. In the context of education, Thorndyke (1961) puts it this way: 'It cannot be too much emphasised that measurement at best provides only information, not judgement'. Gardner (1962) comes near to the theme of the present discussion when he writes: 'A single isolated test score is of little or no value. For a score to have meaning and to be of social or scientific utility, some sort of frame of reference is needed'.

Of course, the measurement process should be efficient. Ideally, the instruments used should measure only what they are supposed to measure, and do so with precision. Instruments used in the physical world tend to approach this ideal, though through familiarity with them we tend to forget how extraordinarily accurate they can be and what fantastic achievements they represent. Those of us concerned with measuring aspects of human behaviour have to be content with much less. In technical terms, our instruments provide measurements whose reliability and validity are imperfect: the inferences we are able to make from these fallible measurements are much less clear-cut. In part, invalidity arises from the difficulty we encounter in describing exactly the attribute in question, and our measurement of it is correspondingly imprecise. Further invalidity arises because of the all but insuperable difficulty we often encounter in attempting to isolate that attribute from a host of extraneous influences which contaminate our measurements. As to unreliability, its sources are legion and to discuss them would take us too far afield.

The need was pointed out earlier for some sort of frame of reference in the interpretation of test scores. In educational measurement, there are, basically, two kinds of reference frame. The first of these involves the use of information gathered from some specifically defined group of individuals called the reference group. In the second, there is no reference group. Instead, the measuring device or test itself provides the reference.

Norm-referenced tests

Tests of the first kind produce measurements which provide information relating a particular individual's performance to that of other individuals in the reference group when the assessment procedure is the same for all. The measurements produced are of various degrees of sophistication: crude marks, ranks, percentiles, grades, standardised scores. The normal or Gaussian curve may be brought into play as, for example, in the American grade point system in which five grades are delimited including, from the first to the fifth respectively, 7, 24, 38, 24 and 7 per cent of the group tested.

Whatever the procedure, and however sophisticated the measure, the basic principle with tests of the first kind is the same: the measures they provide define a continuum of performance ranging from the highest in the group to the lowest, and the measure assigned to a particular member of the group locates his position on that continuum. The group as a whole has a normative function in determining the level and range of performance, and assessment procedures using this principle are accordingly termed *norm-referenced*.

To illustrate, Tom's score on a reading comprehension test places him at the 80th percentile in the reference group (which simply means that his performance on this test is superior to that of 80 per cent of the group's members); while Dick's score places him lower down, perhaps at the 50th percentile. Once the relationship between crude scores and percentiles has been established and tabulated for this test and this reference group, the test can then be administered to other pupils outside the group and their crude scores interpreted as percentiles relating their performances to those of members of the group. For instance, one such pupil, Harry, obtains a crude score which, referred to the table of percentile norms, places him at the 80th percentile, alongside Tom.

Notice that this normative procedure tells us nothing directly about the performance, in *absolute* terms, of any pupil. As a whole, the reference group providing the standard may be 'bright' or 'dull'. The performance of Harry, the pupil from outside the group, was at the 80th percentile in relation to that of pupils in *this* group which happens to be 'dull'. Precisely the same performance on the same test might have relegated Harry to the 65th percentile, had a different and 'brighter' group been chosen as reference group. In short, the information this normative procedure provides about performance is basically relative. What it means in absolute terms must be judged by other means.

Criterion-referenced tests

With the second frame of reference, the interpretation of our test measurements is different. We now enquire whether the pupil has achieved some previously specified criterion performance. We do not report that he ranks seventh in his class; or stands at the 64th percentile in relation to some reference group; or has been placed in grade 2. Instead, we report either that he has, or that he has not, reached a *previously prescribed* level of competence. With either reference frame, the initial information provided by the crude mark is the same; it is the interpretation of this information which differs. To take a simple example where the issue is clear cut, our pupil may have obtained a mark of 16 out of 20 on a test of spelling. Using the first frame, we might say that this performance ranks him above 72 per cent of the members of his class. Using the second, we might say that compared to a level of competence previously defined as at least 18 out of 20, the pupil's achievement in spelling is still unsatisfactory.

Assessment of this second kind, in which the pupil's competence level in some attribute is judged by his performance level on a test designed to measure that attribute, is termed *criterion-referenced*.

Differences between norm- and criterion-referencing

Test theory has been mainly concentrated until relatively recently on the norm-referenced approach: in part because of the pre-occupation of psychologists with trait variability and with individual differences; in part because of the reliance of measurement specialists on the mental test model and the desire of test constructors to build tests that are appropriate in several instructional systems and for various purposes; and in part because of the reluctance or inability of educators to specify their desired goals in terms of observable behaviour.

The distinction between norm-referenced and criterion-referenced tests has important technical implications for the test constructor which will be discussed shortly. Meanwhile, we should note at this point the different *uses* to which these two contrasting approaches to assessment can be put. Norm-referenced assessment procedures are best used in situations where selection is desirable or necessary: for instance, when students are competing for a limited number of university places. Here it is important that the assessment procedure should make possible relative (and, one hopes, valid) comparisons among the students. Criterion-referenced measures, on the other hand, are best used when our interest is in determining whether a student possesses, or does not possess, some particular skill or competence; in identifying his problems; in monitoring his progress through a sequence of tasks; in short, for purposes of diagnosis in both general and specific senses.

It would be idle to deny the importance of the norm-referenced interpretation of test measurements. Often it is useful to know how a student stands in relation to his peers. But in implementing the norm-referenced approach we should be quite clear what we are doing. It is all very well to know that Johnny is top of his class in reading or Suzy's performance in a spelling test places her at the 37th percentile in relation to the reference group on which the test was normed. However, we surely need also to ask: how good is Johnny's class as a whole in reading? Was the reference group used to norm Suzy's test good or poor on the average? When we use a normative procedure we are taking as our reference point whatever happens to be average performance. Unless we keep in mind what we are doing in gearing our tests to the average in this way, we are apt to take it for granted that the average itself is satisfactory. We should remember that normative data simply reflect what is, and not what might be, in a better ordered world. Even the best relative performance may be poor in absolute terms.

The concept of norm-referencing has implications for the test construction procedure. If the results are to be interpreted normatively, the first essential is that they should discriminate clearly and definitely among those tested. Accordingly, in selecting items for the test from the possible pool of items, we accept only those which individually and in concert serve this end. We reject items which themselves do not discriminate, or which, when brigaded with others, do not enhance discrimination.

The different purpose of a criterion-referenced test is reflected in a different construction procedure. In broadest terms, that purpose is to provide information about what students have, or have not, achieved in a particular domain or area of study. Discrimination is no longer important and the test is not built to discriminate.

Because of its different purpose, items may well be incorporated in the criterion-referenced test which would find no place in a norm-referenced test. One reason for rejecting items from a norm-referenced test is that so few of the testees can do them that the items fail to discriminate. In the test constructor's parlance, they are too 'difficult' or have a low 'facility value'. This may be so, but from the criterion-referenced position we should ask two questions. Firstly: does success on these 'difficult' items represent achievement which we ought to expect of the pupils at their present stage of development? And if so, then secondly: *why* do they find these items difficult, and what shall we do about it?

This is the crux of the matter. The criterion-referenced test is designed to help us identify with some confidence the tasks the pupil can perform so that appropriate action can then be taken. Such identification is particularly important, for instance, in individualised instruction. The signal is given for the pupil successful so far to proceed to the next stage, and for remedial measures to be applied to his less successful class-mate.

Let us sum up the distinctions made so far between norm-referenced and criterion-referenced tests.

First, they differ in the *purpose* for which the tests were constructed: for the norm-referenced test, to place the pupil at a point on a continuum determined by his test performance in relation to that of other pupils; for the criterion-referenced test, to place him in a quite different continuum defined by a set of progressive tasks at a point which marks off the tasks he can do from those he cannot yet do.

Second (following from the first), they differ in the *manner* in which they were constructed: for the norm-referenced test, a construction procedure directed at producing an instrument capable of discriminating as widely as possible among the pupils tested, from which follows the rejection of items which do not aid this discrimination; for the criterion-referenced test, inclusion of items representing a continuum of relevant tasks which may or may not include items the norm-referenced test constructor would reject.

Third, they differ in the *use* to which the information derived from the administration of the test is put. The norm-referenced test aids selection in situations where selection is desirable or necessary; helps forecast or predict subsequent success; or again, helps make comparisons among the different sub-groups within a larger group. The criterion-referenced test, pin-points for the teacher the problems encountered by pupils and, more generally, provides information about what each pupil can or cannot do.

In addition to these three, there are two other respects in which the two test styles differ. The fourth difference is that information about the pupil's performance of relevant tasks is more *specific* with the criterion-referenced test than with the norm-referenced test. To take a concrete example, the extent of a pupil's reading ability must be inferred from what he does when confronted with something to read. The constructor of a norm-referenced test will postulate a dimension of 'reading ability', and tailor his test to reveal how far the pupil is along it in relation to other pupils. The scores he obtains in particular parts of the test are of no interest in themselves.

Instead, these part-scores are simply summed to give a total global score. It is across-the-board performance that counts, reflecting the postulate the test constructor started from, namely, a single dimension of 'reading ability'. How well the pupil has done on each of the several parts of the test is of secondary importance.

By contrast, the constructor of a criterion-referenced test will design it so that inferences can be made from the pupil's performance on each one of the several component parts into which the skill of reading can be analysed. These might be, for example, his ability to read aloud without stumbling; to pronounce words intelligibly; to answer questions, either verbally or in writing, designed to show understanding of what he has read; to react emotionally to a poem he reads, and so on. It is now the part-scores reflecting performance on each of the facets of the skill that matter, the global score being largely irrelevant. Though improbable, it may happen that different pupils turn in quite different patterns of part-scores adding up to similar, or even identical global scores—a situation of which a norm-referenced test would take no account. These 'profiles' would be of the essence, however, for a criterion-referenced test designed to tell us whether each individual's performance on each separate part of the test does or does not reach a previously defined point of acceptability.

The fifth respect in which norm-referenced and criterion-referenced tests differ is the manner in which the information provided by them is *generalisable*. In the case of a norm-referenced test, generalisation is associated with validity defined as the extent to which the test measures what it is supposed to measure. Let us imagine an experiment in which the norm-referenced test is administered to a group of pupils already divided, maybe in rough-and-ready fashion, into good, middling and poor readers on the basis of their teacher's judgement. Global scores on the test are found to categorise the pupils similarly, that is, the test scores confirm the teacher's judgements. The test scores thus appear to be valid measures in respect of *this* teacher's judgements about *this* group of pupils. The whole experiment is now repeated with a similarly constructed test, though of different content which is administered to a *different* group of pupils categorised for reading ability by a *different* teacher. Again the test scores confirm the teacher's judgements. Further replication of the experiment with different tests, different pupil groups, and different teachers produces similar results. In the light of this, we feel encouraged to generalise in two ways. There *does* appear to be a general dimension which we may call 'reading ability' and on which teachers in general can judge pupils in general; and there *is* a general family of tests which furnish valid information about this general ability.

The information provided by a criterion-referenced test is generalisable in quite a different manner. The test is designed to tell us which relevant tasks the pupil can perform and which he cannot. Its items must therefore present examples of all such tasks and his performance on these items must be generalisable to the whole skill domain they represent.

It follows that before the test can be constructed, the skill must be analysed into its component parts, aspects, sub-skills, call them what you will. The items included in the test must be adequate examplars of the tasks which such analysis identifies and which the pupil must be able to accomplish before we judge him to have mastered the skill in question.

But this is easier said than done. Manifestly, the domain may be large and difficult to map, and choosing examples turn out to be quite a problem. How do we know— in some cases can we ever know—the extent of the domain? Given the domain, what sampling procedure should we use in selecting items for inclusion in the test? Are all examples equally useful; or are some more potent than others in providing information about a pupil's mastery of the domain? On what basis should we make crucial decisions about 'can' or 'cannot' which, as said earlier, give the green light to one but not to another?

Criterion-referencing—a closer look

At this point we leave norm-referenced tests to take care of themselves—which they are perfectly capable of doing. They have been with us for a long time and have the support of considerable educational and psychometric theory. We turn now to a discussion of some of the problems that manifest themselves on taking a closer look at tests of the criterion-referenced genre.

The preceding paragraphs would have served, up to the end of the sixties, as an outline statement of how the art of criterion-referenced testing was generally seen at that time. Following Glaser's (1963) seminal article, these tests, and their link with the concept of mastery, were generally welcomed as educationally and philosophically more acceptable than their norm-referenced counterparts. It was more important to know the pupil's standing in relation to the tasks to be accomplished than vis-a-vis his peers. Ebel (1972), commenting on this surge of interest during the sixties, writes: 'Some articles . . . suggested that education had been wandering for more than forty years in the wilderness of norm-referenced measurements and that a shift to criterion-referenced measurements could lead education to its promised land'.

During the last decade or so the attitude towards criterion-referenced testing has become less euphoric. Ebel (1972), who from the outset had counselled caution, concluded that 'Criterion-referenced measures do not tell us all, or even the most important parts, of what we need to know about the educational achievements of our students'.

'Domain'-referencing

As always, one source of difficulty has been lack of agreement over the definition of terms. The briefest glance at some of the plethora of articles on criterion-referenced tests—a recent count is some 600 to date—indicates that there are many different ideas about what these tests are and can do. Even the word 'criterion' gives rise to confusion. For many, it refers to a standard of performance, a minimum proficiency level, or a cut-off score. However, there seems to be increasing concensus that 'criterion' should be taken to refer to a *domain of behaviours* measuring some objective or skill. Hence the definition put forward by Popham (1975): 'A criterion-referenced test is used to ascertain an individual's status (referred to as a domain score) with respect to a well-defined behaviour domain'. By hindsight, 'domain-referenced' would have led to less confusion than 'criterion-referenced' had it been adopted earlier, and would certainly have expressed more clearly what the most influential early writers, such as Glaser (1963) and Popham and Husek (1969), had in mind.

Mastery-continuum and state models

Equally, the term 'mastery' has more connotations than one. Consonant with the concept of 'domain-referenced' tests is the use of such tests to assign examinees to mastery *states*, or *categories*. There is no set limit to the number of categories; in particular, there are not necessarily (though there may be) just two, representing respectively 'mastery' and 'non-mastery'. Viewed in this way, mastery is seen as a continuously distributed ability or set of abilities, and an individual's test performance places him at some point on this continuum. By implication, this *continuum* model (as it is called), allows for several different degrees of mastery. Nevertheless, at some expense to logic, an individual is often termed a 'master' only if his performance equals or exceeds some prescribed lower bound on this continuum.

By contrast with the *continuum* model, the *state* model conceptualises mastery as an all-or-none description of the pupil's learning state in respect of a specified content domain. Davis and Diamond (1974) remark tartly: ' "Partial mastery" is as self-contradictory as "partial uniqueness" '. They continue: 'The term "mastery", therefore, should be used to describe the status of only those examinees who, it may be inferred, can mark correctly all the items in the population of which the subset that makes up a criterion-referenced test is a representative sample'. Proponents of this view maintain it to be the logical outcome of their educational philosophy: if pupils fail to achieve certain objectives, the blame must be laid on an educational process insensitive to their individual needs and characteristics. With a properly devised programme substantially all students (90 per cent according to Bloom) could be brought to a mastery state.

It does seem that the state model is more appropriate than the continuum model in the context of mastery learning as advocated by Bloom *et al.* (1971) and, though very differently, by Keller. Both strategies make use of units to be mastered successively. With Bloom, the pupils remain together in their instruction; no-one in the group moves on to the next unit until all group members have achieved mastery of the present one. Bloom maintains that the inevitably slow start is compensated for later by accelerated learning of the less gifted who are increasingly motivated by more secure understanding of the earlier units. In the long run the group performance achieved is characterised by a higher mean and lower scatter than would have been the case with more traditional learning procedures. Although the educational growth of the brighter pupils is almost certainly retarded, this is seen as a sacrifice acceptable in a group teaching system which purports to minimise sacrifice overall. As to the other extreme, one of the proponents of this strategy for mastery learning, J. K. Smith (1977), remarks: 'If students are not capable of learning the course content, then they should not be on the course'.

By contrast, in the Keller Personalised System of Instruction (PSI), pupils work on the units individually and at their own pace, taking the unit tests when they believe they are ready. They must reach a certain level of mastery on the test before going on to the next unit.

Despite their differences in strategy, the Bloom and Keller procedures have it in common that no pupil goes on to the next unit until he has displayed mastery of the present one in the appropriate test. Since each unit is a relatively small step, and hence likely to be relatively homogeneous in educational content, it should not be too difficult, on the face of it, to analyse this content in order to develop appropriate tests on a unit-by-unit basis and to interpret the test results *seriatim* in terms of mastery or non-mastery in accordance with the state model (see page 10). Theoretically, of course, with this all-or-none model, the shape of the acquisition 'curve' for the behaviour being measured is a step function with a slope of zero at all but one point. In practice, the degree of perfection the model proposes is unobtainable in this imperfect world. Hence, to the question whether or not an individual has achieved mastery the answer is often an intuitive one: perfect performance is not demanded, but there is an intuitively reasonable assurance that those pupils who have reached a prescribed level have achieved a mastery state. Alternatively, in quest of objectivity, decision models have been proposed which take into account factors giving rise to measurement error. More will be said on this issue later.

Meanwhile, we may note that the unit-by-unit mastery tests, state model based, that characterise both Bloom and Keller strategies are those familiar to most of us as *formative* tests. At the end of the course, all pupils will take a criterion-referenced *summative* test, covering all the material the pupils have previously encountered in the unit sequence. This summative test is almost certainly more heterogeneous in content and broader in scope than any of the specifically unit-orientated tests. It seems therefore reasonable to classify it as a domain-referenced test conforming to the continuum model rather than the state model; and there is no reason why this summative test should not be used to assign pupils to one or other of several categories delimited by cut-off scores fixed in accordance with the teacher's judgement.

Some problems

On page 39 we left hanging the question of how to analyse a skill into its component parts in order to determine the item content for inclusion in a test of that skill.

The task of identifying what is to be measured in a criterion-referenced test is not simple; nor is it the only task which presents problems in the criterion-referenced area. Consider, for example, the end-of-unit mastery tests which are part of the Bloom and Keller instructional procedures. On the face of it, these should be easy to construct. Individually, each will be geared to a limited and fairly specific instructional objective and probably be short and relatively homogeneous in content. In practice, the simplicity is illusory. Each test must seek to distinguish between those pupils who have, and those who have not, achieved sufficient mastery of the current unit's content to be able to tackle the next unit with a fair prospect of success. To put it slightly differently, a pupil's mastery of one unit must be a reliable and valid predictor of his mastery of the next. Skill and judgement are called for in several directions: in initial curriculum planning, the need to take account of factors, both logical and psychological, in order to ease transition from unit to unit; in the actual construction of test items; in checking that the items so constructed do indeed add up to a test which is a valid predictor in the sense referred to above; and in determining cut-off points which minimise errors in assigning pupils to mastery or non-mastery states.

These problems have their counterparts when we move from the state model to the continuum model, that is, to domain-referenced testing. One major problem of course, is that of domain specification, for which the ideal requirements are:

1. All the items which could be written from the content domain to be tested must be written (or known) in advance;

2. The process for selecting items for inclusion in the test must be based on a random or stratified sampling procedure.

It is not impossible, of course, for these requirements to be met. For example, given the digits 1–9, there are 45 possible two-digit addition items, or 81 if order of presentation of the digits is taken into account. Or, starting from the same array of digits, there are 45 subtraction items with non-negative answers. In these cases, the statistical canons would be observed if random sampling were used to produce tests of, say 10 items. As another example, Ebel (1962) constructed vocabulary tests from a 'population' of words from a particular dictionary. The tests each contained 100 items based on words chosen in accordance with a tightly specified sampling procedure; and the item format was equally tightly specified (the format adopted was a 'matching' between words and definitions presented alongside each other in 'scrambled' orders).

These examples serve to underscore a major weakness in domain specification and item generation: the ideal requirements are likely to be met only with highly structured subject matter areas such as those exemplified. Perhaps it is no accident that the areas in which mastery learning has proved most successful include mathematics, science and foreign languages. It has been least successful in English, composition, social studies, literature, reading, and so on.

It has to be recognised that fulfilment of the ideal requirements is seldom practicable. In the first place, assuming that it is possible to specify numerous objectives in detail, we may find that within a single domain they display considerable heterogeneity. Sub-domains (as we may call them) may be so numerous that unless the whole test is to become unreasonably long, each corresponding subtest must consist of too few items to allow of secure inferences about pupils' mastery states.

In the second place, how often can we assume that specifying objectives in detail is possible? Sometimes, maybe, at elementary levels. At higher levels the process of specification may get out of hand. In sampling from an undefined or under-defined universe we run the risk of bias and hence of faulty inferences about the pupils' wider control of the area. This is, of course, a familiar problem with which we are faced whenever we construct even the most 'objective' of tests and which we solve as best we can.

However, the assumption that objectives can be specified in detail, even in principle, is often untenable. What kind of detailed specification is possible, for example, when the course is English Literature for students at university level? Here we enter the broad realms of understanding, appreciation and criticism within which, it could be argued, any attempt to pin-point specific objectives would produce a travesty of education. As Ebel (1972) points out: 'For knowledge and understanding consist of a complex fabric which owes its strength and beauty to an infinity of tiny fibres of relationship. Knowledge does not come in discrete chunks that can be defined and identified separately'.

Ebel is sceptical about the claims made for criterion-referenced tests as against their norm-referenced counterparts on several grounds. Granting that they can tell us what a person can or cannot do, he does not accept the claim that they do so in absolute terms. 'Excellence or deficiency are necessarily relative concepts', he points out (page 145). Moreover, as an educationist he doubts the wisdom as well as the practicability of specifying objectives in great detail. He acknowledges, of course, that teachers should think hard about what they are teaching, but not to the extent of listing them *in extenso*, atomistically, so to speak. The good teacher, which for Ebel means the flexible and opportunistic teacher, would be hampered by such a list. 'Why', he asks, 'should he (the teacher) labour to translate all these detailed elements of achievement into a statement of objectives? If he should do so, how could he actually keep such a detailed array of statements in mind while teaching? And if he were to manage such a *tour de force*, how formal, rigid and dull his teaching would become'.

'Cut-off' scores

We now turn to another problem associated with the concept of criterion-referenced testing. 'Passing' on such a test frequently implies reaching some previously determined minimal acceptable performance. It is assumed that some educational decision is conditional on whether the pupil reaches, or does not reach, an adequate proficiency standard on a test which samples the domain concerned. How should this proficiency standard be defined?

In the first place, we should reject out of hand the all too frequent practice of assigning a particular passing score or pass-mark purely on grounds of tradition. To fix a pass-mark at, say, 65 per cent for each and every domain on which the pupil is tested takes no account of the relative importances of these different domains. The teacher may judge it essential for the pupil to display complete or near mastery in one domain, but not essential in another. Pass-marks should reflect these differences, and a pass-mark owing its origin solely to tradition cannot do this.

A procedure which at first sight seems reasonable is to determine in advance what proportion of students should pass, and fix the pass-mark accordingly. However, whether an individual pupil passes or not then depends in large measure on the competence of others taking the test. The claim that passing depends on the pupil achieving some predetermined standard, which is basic to the concept of criterion-referenced testing, cannot then be maintained.

A more acceptable procedure is to base the pass-mark on expert judgement of the items in the test. This might be done by first arranging the items in groups. In order to pass, the pupil must provide acceptable answers to *all* the items in one group; to a smaller proportion of those in another; a smaller proportion still of those in a third; and so on.

A routine for accomplishing this procedure is provided by Angoff (1971): '. . . ask each judge to state the *probability* that the "minimally acceptable person" would answer the question correctly. In effect, the judges would think of a number of minimally acceptable persons, instead of only one such person, and estimate the proportion of minimally acceptable persons who would answer each item correctly. The sum of these probabilities, or proportions, would then represent the minimally acceptable score'.

For instance, in a four-item* test, the judges might decide that item 1 must be passed by every minimally acceptable student (probability = 1); item 2 by 80 per cent of such students (probability = 0·8); item 3 by 70 per cent (probability = 0·7); and item 4 by 60 per cent (probability = 0·6). The sum of these probabilities, 3·1 (or just under 78 per cent), is the minimally acceptable score.

Somewhat similar, in that subjective judgement is involved, is a method proposed by Ebel (1972). The minimum passing score is arrived at by a consideration of the items' characteristics along two dimensions: relevance and difficulty. In his example, four relevance categories are used—Essential, Important, Acceptable and Questionable. There are three difficulty levels—Easy, Medium and Hard. All items or questions are classified in the 4×3 grid on the basis of raters' judgements as to the relevance and difficulty of these items or questions for the minimally qualified examinee. Judgements are also made, for each cell in the table, regarding the proportions of items in the cell that the minimally qualified examinee should be able to answer. The number of items in each cell is then 'weighted' by the corresponding proportion and the weighted sum across all cells is the lowest passing score.

More recently, Berk (1976) has suggested an empirical method of choosing a 'cut-off' score which makes use of the response data from two groups of examinees, one 'instructed', the other 'uninstructed'. It is assumed that all members of the 'instructed' group are masters, and all members of the 'uninstructed' group non-masters. The test, administered to both groups, dichotomises each about a cutting-score C. This score divides the 'instructed' group into 'true masters' (TM) and 'false non-masters' (FM); and the 'uninstructed' group into 'true non-masters' (TN) and 'false masters' (FM). The TM and TN categories are regarded as correctly classified, the others as incorrectly. The optimum value of the cutting score is that which maximises the proportions of correct classifications, TM and TN.

The procedure has an appealing simplicity, but its usefulness depends on how valid the initial assumption is that all in the instructed group are true masters and all in the uninstructed group true non-masters.

A factor to be taken into account in fixing the passing level is the effect on future learning or, more generally, the educational consequences. If the level is set too low, pupils may be exposed subsequently to concepts or skills for which they are not yet ready. Setting it too high may hold back pupils from materials they are in fact equipped to master. Light could be thrown on this aspect of the problem by a follow-up study in which different groups of pupils earning different scores on the test are compared for their later performances on some subsequent criterion. Block's (1972) studies of this sort with students of matrix algebra suggest a 'passing score' of 95 per cent to maximise learning as represented by cognitive criteria, and 85 per cent for learning as characterised by affective criteria.

Where information about educational consequences is lacking, the guide-lines suggested by Garvin (1971) are useful: 'If on the basis of a logical analysis of the subject matter and the extant instructional system, the knowledges and skills are

---

*An actual test would of course contain more than four items. However, the principle is the same.

seen as fundamental or prerequisite to future learning, then a high proficiency level is required. A lower passing score can be tolerated when the material is not seen as completing a necessary link in the development of some more complex concept or skill, especially if the idea will be covered again in the curriculum. . . . Tests of performance not viewed as pre-requisite for future learning should not have passing scores'.

Also to be taken into account are the psychological effects on the pupil. The consequences of fixing too high a passing score may be boredom, loss of motivation and damage to self-concept in pupils who do not reach it. Too low a passing score may produce psychological confusion in pupils who are moved too rapidly through the curriculum.

Errors of sampling

A difficulty not always recognised is that associated with sampling from the domain. To illustrate the nature of the problem, let us suppose that we are constructing a vocabulary test. The pupils are supposed to know a large target vocabulary which has been listed. We propose to pass only those who 'know' 80 per cent or more of the target vocabulary. The content of our test is based on a sample of, say, ten words drawn at random from the complete list. On the basis that knowledge of 80 per cent or better of the words in the target vocabulary is acceptable, we propose to pass pupils who score 80 per cent or better on the test items, that is, who score 8, 9 or 10.

But what actually happens? Consider Tom, who does in fact know exactly 80 per cent of the words in the target vocabulary. We might expect him to score 8 on the 10-item test which is a random sample of the vocabulary. But the sample of words contained in the test may be a 'lucky draw' for him: he may know 9 or even all 10 of the words and score accordingly. The probability of his scoring 9 or 10 is in fact nearly 38 per cent. Of course, this does not affect the issue for Tom—he rightly passes anyhow. But the luck of the draw may go in the other direction: he may know fewer than 8 of the words in the test. The probability of this happening, in which case he wrongly fails, is 32 per cent. To put the matter differently, we can predict in advance that of a large group of pupils who, like Tom, all know exactly 80 per cent of the target vocabulary, we shall rightly classify 68 per cent as passing and wrongly classify 32 per cent as failing if we fix the minimally acceptable pass-mark as 8 out of 10.

Next consider Dick, who knows 90 per cent of the target vocabulary and who therefore ought to pass handsomely. For him the luck of the draw means that the probability of his passing is 74 per cent and of his failing, 26 per cent. In other words, we shall know that of all pupils who, like Dick, know 90 per cent of the vocabulary, we shall wrongly fail over one-quarter by fixing the pass-mark at 8 out of 10.

Next, Harry, who knows only 70 per cent of the target vocabulary and who therefore ought to fail. The luck of the draw may favour him and he might know 8, 9 or even all 10 of the words in the test. The total probability that this will happen, that he will be wrongly passed, is about 38 per cent.

46

Finally Bill, who knows only 60 per cent of the vocabulary, has a 16 per cent probability of wrongly passing.

Mis-classification of this sort is bound to happen. Wherever we choose to fix the pass-mark, some who should pass will fail, while others who should fail will pass, for no other reason than the vagaries of random sampling. The size of the effect depends on the length of the test: with a short test, of course, the mis-classification will be more extensive than with a longer one.

Reliability and validity

The reliability of a test procedure is defined as the precision with which the procedure measures whatever it does measure (which may or may not be what it purports to measure). In the context of norm-referenced tests it is expressed as the correlation or degree of correspondence between scores on one form of the procedure and scores on another form, actual or conceptual, the two forms being equivalent in that both have been developed in the same way and according to the same principles.

Common to all the correlational devices used to assign a numerical value to the reliability—product moment, rank, biserial, phi, and so on—is the requirement that the test procedure shall generate a spread or scatter of scores. This requirement follows from the basic definition or a reliability coefficient as the ratio of the variance of the 'true' scores we are attempting to measure to the 'observed' scores which are the more or less close approximation we have to content ourselves with in practice. The operative word here is *variance*.

By virtue of the procedures used in constructing a norm-referenced test, the scores it produces characteristically vary across the individuals in the group tested. Hence, in estimating the reliability of a norm-referenced test, there is no problem in using the standard formulae.

However, the help these formulae have to offer in the context of criterion-referenced testing is limited to say the least. Tests of this kind are not built to discriminate among the testees and in fact may not do so. A teacher would positively welcome a test's zero discrimination among his pupils if the test results were to signal complete success on his part and theirs in the achievement of some educational objective; and if a retest a week later produced a similar happy result, the inapplicability of standard procedures in describing the perfect correspondence between these replications would not unduly diminish his satisfaction.

Nevertheless, some reliability estimate is manifestly desirable. Not surprisingly, attempts have been made to apply to criterion-referenced tests the concepts of classical test theory already worked out in the norm-referenced context. Livingston (1972) has suggested a generalisation of our ideas about variability of test scores which brings the concepts of reliability and validity to bear in criterion-referenced testing—even with tests which produce minimum discrimination (in its usual sense) among those tested. Briefly, Livingston advocates measuring score deviations from the pre-determined cut-off score instead of from the average of all scores, as is standard practice. The further this average is from the cut-off score, the most reliable the scores appear to be. Livingston's procedure gives a determinate result even in the case where all testees have obtained the same score, so that score variance is zero; in this case the application of classical test theory in estimating the test reliability would have led to an indeterminate result*.

However, Livingston's development is not without its critics. Harris (1972) points out that the standard error of measurement (which, when all is said and done, is the key statistic in reliability estimation) comes out the same whether derived by application of straight-forward classical theory or by Livingston's modification of it.

Estimation of standard error of measurement seems to have become the focus for recent discussion and research proposals. A test's standard error of measurement is relatively invariant across different samples of testees, in contrast to reliability estimates, which can vary considerably. The standard error of measurement is therefore useful in interpreting test measurements, whether norm-referenced or criterion-referenced. Moreover, there is increasing interest in estimating the standard errors of measurement of scores obtained by individual persons; these errors are often found to differ from person to person. They are more informative and probably more useful to the test user than the test standard error which is a kind of average† of these individual errors of measurement. Various procedures have been proposed, too technical for discussion here. Those interested are referred to Cronbach *et al.* (1972); Millman (1974); Hambleton *et al.* (1976); Brenner and Kane (1977); and Wright (1977).

In estimating the predictive validity of a criterion-referenced test, the classical model suffers from the same deficiency as that already noted in connection with the estimation of test reliability: the standard correlational procedures are seldom appropriate where there is no built-in score variance in either the predictor or the criterion, or both.

Nevertheless, with mastery test characterised by cut-off scores, the standard 'prediction' procedure is still possible, as Berk (1976) points out. The test is administered to a group which includes both 'masters' and 'non-masters'. The validity of the test's discrimination between these two subgroups is estimated by the non-parametric correlation coefficient phi.

In the main, however, discussion of the validity of criterion-referenced tests has been directed towards establishing or enhancing their content validity. The quality of a criterion-referenced test depends on the quality of its items; and this in turn depends on the extent to which item content reflects the domain from which the items were derived.

An obvious procedure in establishing item content validity involves judgements made of tests items by content specialists who look for correspondence between what they judge each item to measure and the domain it purports to measure. Provided that the domain specification can be clearly written in the first place,

---

*In classical test theory, reliability is defined as the ratio of true score variance to observed score variance. In the case cited, this ratio is 0/0, and hence is indeterminate.
†This statement is completely accurate if for 'standard error' we substitute its square, 'error variance'. The test 'error variance of measurement' is the average of individual 'error variances of measurement' of scores obtained by all persons taking the test.

content specialists can be asked, for example, to rate the test items relative to this specification on a scale of +1 (yes), 0 (undecided) and −1 (no). Final selection of items is then based on the consensus judgement of these experts.

Cronbach (1971) has suggested a test construction procedure in which validity is built in and checked for at the outset. Two teams of equally competent item-writers could work independently in developing criterion-referenced tests starting from the same definition of relevant content, and working to the same rules for sampling, reviewing, try-out and interpretation. The equivalence of the tests could be checked by administering both to the same group of examinees. 'If the universe description and the sampling are ideally refined, the first and second tests will be entirely equivalent. Any person's score will be the same on both test within the limits of sampling error'.

Concluding comments

The fact that there are still these unsolved or only partially solved problems points to the need for more fundamental research into the rationale and construction of criterion-referenced tests. In the research race they have come off badly in comparison with norm-referenced tests. The principles underlying both are basically equally simple. But while test theory and test development on the norm-referenced side of the fence have reached a high pitch of sophistication, we are still feeling our way on the criterion-referenced side. For nearly half a century the norm-referenced preserve has been a favourite stamping-ground for educationists, psychologists, test specialists and amateur statisticians. Some of them are now beginning to jump over the fence, and not before time.

It must be recognised that each approach, norm-referenced and criterion-referenced, poses problems in use. The whole ethic of norm-referenced tests has come under attack in some quarters because they are alleged to promote harmful competition and foster invidious inter-person comparisons. On a less emotive plane, the limited nature of the information they provide, whether rank, percentile, standardised score or whatever, cannot be gainsaid. 'It is unfortunate,' writes Ebel (1962), 'that some specialists in measuring educational achievement have seemed to imply that knowing how many of his peers a student can excel is more important than knowing what he can do to excel them'. To which one might add: 'and how well he can do it.'

This is not to deny the value of norm-referencing. To quote Ebel again: 'To be meaningful any test scores must be related to test content *as well as* to the scores of other examinees'. To know that a person is outstanding in some field is often enough to establish the nature and quality of his achievement in that field. To know, for instance, that an athlete ranks third in the world list of 1500 metre specialists is to know also that he can cover the distance in something under four minutes. In the educational field, we do often know enough about course content and level to make some judgement of the amount of each pupil's knowledge or degree of ability from his position in class.

However, in all probability, a better judgement of pupils' knowledge and degree of ability will emerge from a criterion-referenced test specifically designed to measure these attributes. The major problems here are: the difficulty encountered in detailed mapping of a probably large domain; and of writing tests which are unbiased samples of that domain and are still of practicable length.

Problems also arise in estimating the reliability and validity of tests used for this purpose. In measuring reliability and validity, the standard procedures which depend on variability of test scores, are of limited use. The temptation to inject variability by deliberately selecting best-discriminating items must be resisted. There is difficulty enough in achieving unbiased sampling from a hazily-defined domain without exacerbating the difficulty by consciously adding to the bias.

It is appropriate to conclude this discussion of norm-referenced and criterion-referenced tests by citing an example of the use of both approaches in a single examination. Tharu (1973) argues that a combination of both approaches can be more efficient than either separately. Using the English Language paper set at the Indian High School/PUC level as an example, he argues in favour of dividing the content into two parts or stages. Stage 1 is 'designed specifically to test mastery of the points considered as minimum essentials'. Stage II is intended to 'discriminate among degrees of mastery of the advanced skills'. Stage I is virtually a criterion-referenced test. It consists of several blocks of items, within each of which the items are all aimed at testing the same elementary skill, while different blocks test different skills. For example, the first block in Tharu's illustrative test contains eight items all testing mastery of personal pronouns; the second, eight items all concerned with WH-words (who, where, when, which); and so on.

Casting a test in this format, with homogeneity within blocks and heterogeneity among blocks, is of course not new. The format has been used in many tests, especially those used for diagnostic purposes. The use Tharu makes of it, which has to do with the pass-fail decision, is perhaps less familiar. To pass in Stage I, the student must display a considerable degree of 'mastery', both within and among blocks. Specifically, Tharu suggests, firstly, that the minimum acceptable or 'Pass' performance on each individual block should be 75 per cent—anything below that is a 'Fail' and counts zero; and secondly, that this minimum should be obtained in not less than 80 per cent of all the blocks. The student not achieving this previously specified level of performance fails not only on Stage I, but overall. Any marks he obtains on Stage II do not count. If he passes Stage I, the final decision on *overall* pass depends entirely on his performance on Stage II. In effect, a pass on Stage I is simply a passport to Stage II and carries no bonus in the shape of marks. All students going on to Stage II do so from the same starting-point.

The content of Stage II is more exacting. It includes, *inter alia*, more difficult vocabulary and structures, reading comprehension and essay writing. The marks are used to rank the students—that is, the norm-referenced approach takes over at this stage.

Tharu's main objective in structuring the test in this way is to rationalise the Pass-Fail decision. He points out that with the examination as currently constructed and marked, all marks obtained, on whatever part of the test, are 'as good as' each other. A difference of 4 marks in elementary vocabulary 'counts' just as much as a difference of 4 marks in much more advanced reading comprehension or essay-writing. Accordingly, different students may achieve the same pass-mark in all sorts of ways, some of which, when scrutinised closely, may merit a pass, while others do not. Tharu points to Carroll's dictum that the purpose of testing is to provide information to help make intelligent decisions about possible courses of action. What kind of information, asks Tharu, does a pass-mark provide when it masks so much variability in its make-up? What sort of intelligent decision is possible on such a basis?

Tharu contends that the two-stage structure he proposes will reduce the gamble for overall pass. It will exclude at the outset those students with insufficient grasp of basic essentials for their probably meagre performances at a more advanced level to have any meaning. For those going on to Stage II, the mark-equivalent principle does operate: '. . . the occurrence of highly irregular profiles is unlikely. Few students are likely to do well in some questions and very badly in others'. Consequently, differences among students thrown up by Stage II are more meaningful and helpful, in Carroll's sense, in reaching intelligent decisions.

References

Angoff, W. H. 'Scales, norms and equivalent scores' in R. L. Thorndyke (Ed.) *Educational Measurement*. Washington: American Council on Education, 1971.

Berk, R. A. 'Determination of optimal cutting-score in criterion-referenced measurement'. 1976 *J. Exper. Ed.*, *45*, 4–9.

Block, H. H. 'Student learning and the setting of mastery standards'. *Educational Horizons*, 1972, *50*, 183–190.

Bloom, B. S., Hastings, J. T. and Madaus, G. F. *Handbook on Formative and Summative Evaluation of Student Learning*. New York: McGraw-Hill, 1971.

Brennan, R. L. and Kane, M. T. 'An index of dependability for mastery tests'. *J. Educ. Meas.*, 1977, *14*, 277–289.

Cronbach, L. J. 'Test validation' in R. L. Thorndyke (Ed.) *Educational Measurement* (2nd Edn.). Washington: American Council on Education, 1971.

Cronbach, L. J., Glaser, G. C., Nanda, H. and Rajaratuam, N. *The Dependability of Behavioural Measurements: Theory of Generalizability for Scores and Profiles*. New York: Wiley, 1972.

Davis, F. B. and Diamond, J. J. 'The preparation of criterion-referenced tests?' in Harris, Alkin and Popham (Eds.) *Problems in Criterion-referenced Measurement*. Los Angeles: UCLA Graduate School of Education, Centre for the Study of Evaluation 1974.

Ebel, R. L. 'Content standard test scores'. *Educ. and Psych. Meas.*, 1962, *22*, (1), 11–17.

Ebel, R. L. *'Essentials of Educational Measurement'*. New Jersey: Prentice-Hall, 1972.

Ebel, R. L. 'Some limitations of criterion-referenced measurement' in Bracht, Hopkins and Stanley (Eds.) *Perspectives in Educational and Psychological Measurement*. New Jersey: Prentice-Hall, 1972.

Gardner, E. G. 'Normative standardised scores'. *J. Ed. and Psych. Meas.*, 1962, *22* (1), 7–14.

Garvin, A. D. 'The applicability of criterion-referenced measurement by content area and level' in W. J. Popham (Ed.) *Criterion-referenced Measurement: an Introduction*. New Jersey: Educational Technology Publication, 1971.

Glaser, G. R. 'Instructional technology and the measurement of learning outcomes'. *Amer. Psych.*, 1963, *18*, 519–521.

Hambleton, R. K., Hutten, L. R. and Swaminathan, H. 'A comparison of several methods for assessing student mastery in objective-based instructional projects'. *J. Exp. Ed.*, 1976, *45*, 57–64.

Harris, C. W. 'An interpretation of Livingston's reliability coefficient for criterion-referenced tests'. *J. Educ. Meas.*, 1972, *9*, 27–29.

Keller, F. S. 'Goodbye, Teacher . . .'. *J. Behavioural Analysis*, *1*, 79–89.

Livingston, S. A. 'Criterion-referenced application of classical test theory'. *J. Educ. Meas.*, 1972, *9*, 13–26.

Millman, J. 'Criterion-referenced measurement' in W. J. Popham (Ed.) *Evaluation in Education: Current Applications*. Berkeley, Cal.: McCutchan Pub. Co., 1974.

Popham, W. J. *Educational Evaluation*. New Jersey: Prentice-Hall, 1975.

Smith, J. K. *Perspectives in Mastery Learning and Mastery Testing*. ERIC/TM Report 63, 1977.

Tharu, J. 'Rationalising the pass-fail decision'. Occasional Paper. 1973. Hyderabad: Central Institute for English and Foreign Languages.

Thorndyke, R. L. and Hagen, E. *Measurement and evaluation in Psychology and Education*. New York: Wiley, 1961.

Wright, B. D. 'Solving measurement problems with the Rasch model'. *J. Educ. Meas.*, 1977, *14* (2), 97–115.

ITEM BANKING

The Scottish Certificate of Education Examination Board has been using objective testing techniques for several years in certain subject examinations and many teachers have used similar techniques for school-based assessment in both primary and secondary schools. The writing and editing of items is not easy and teachers have banded together, sometimes with the help of a College of Education, sometimes a Local Authority Adviser, to produce a bank of items upon which all could draw in preparing school-based tests. The Examination Board has also lent a hand and has produced collections of items for mathematics and the sciences covering the first few years of secondary education which it has issued to schools. A recent evaluation of the Integrated Science scheme in use in Scotland has produced another bank of items now published and available for use by teachers. Other projects, such as the development of methods of assessing pupils' attainments in integrated craft work, and others in modern languages, home economics and geography may also result in collections of tests and test materials which will be made available to teachers to use as they wish in the preparation of their own test instruments. While most of these collections have been pre-tested and item statistics are usually made available, these necessarily refer to the particular audience with which the tests have been used. A teacher using any material on a differently constituted audience has little to help him to predict likely outcomes or to compare performance of his group with other comparable groups. Latent Trait Modelling has changed this. It is claimed for this statistical approach that items can be calibrated for difficulty level in a way which is sample free. Such a technique, if it works, makes it possible to consider item-banking on a much bigger scale.

The Department has financed two projects of Research and Development, the one attempting to produce a bank of items to test the mathematical skills of primary children of all ages and abilities, the other to perform a similar task for the less able mathematicians in the third and fourth years of secondary school (the potential Foundation level participants). Mr Alastair Pollitt, who has succeeded Dr Pilliner, the author of the preceding paper, as Assistant Director of Godfrey Thomson Unit is responsible for the primary project. In his paper he draws on his experience in attempting to construct the bank to outline methods, benefits and difficulties, in what is a new venture for Scotland. He gives a relatively simple exposition of the latent trait model (Rasch model) which he uses and this will be of considerable interest to many readers.

Some authors claim that it is possible to use similar statistical models to categorise polychotomous items such as English interpretations, extended answer questions in all subjects, and even open-ended essay type questions. If we are to consider the possibility of external certification for all pupils in the future and include within this an element of internal, and possibly continuous, assessment, then some means will be needed to ensure both the quality of instruments used and some recognised standard of difficulty for each level involved. Are well constructed and calibrated item banks likely to be an aid in making each internal assessment easily standardised for external certification purposes? At primary level, are well prepared item banks a useful resource with which to prepare the diagnostic tests necessary to ensure that pupils are mastering what they are supposed to master? Are all subjects susceptible to item banking techniques?

A.W.J.

Item Banking

A. B. Pollitt

Examining is not a simple business. An examination consists of a set of questions which ought to have the following properties:

1. All parts of the syllabus should be represented by an appropriate number of questions;

2. Each part should contain questions of an appropriate range of difficulty;

3. All the questions should be 'fair' to the candidates receiving them;

4. All the questions should be 'good', in that the more able candidates should be more likely to get them right;

5. The examination as a whole should spread the candidates out to the required extent and discriminate particularly at any pass/fail or inter-grade level.

Writing an examination to fit these specifications, and checking that it does, is expensive and time-consuming. Item banks were initially designed to make examination construction easier; they are evolving into complete measurement systems.

1. What is an Item Bank?

Essentially an item bank is an aid for test constructors. One may be used at any educational level from nursery school to adult college, and for any testing from informal classroom assessment to national or professional certificate examination. A bank contains a large number of questions, which may have been obtained from a variety of sources, but which have all been tested and have all passed certain psychometric criteria. They are 'good' test questions, all discriminating between high and low ability candidates, and a user may select for his test any particular set of items, according to his own needs for curricular content and difficulty. At the very least he is saved the chore of writing questions; at best he is also saved the chores of pre-testing and calibrating them.

There are some words whose usage must be clarified.

Items and Questions. Item banking began (in an informal way) after the introduction of objective testing procedures into examinations. Experience showed that good objective items—that is, questions which have one and only one right answer and are able to discriminate adequately amongst a group of candidates—are difficult and time-consuming to produce and require expensive pre-testing before they can be used with confidence. It seemed to make sense, therefore, to collect these items and to share them with other examiners. Objective tests lend themselves to statistical analysis, and in particular to attempts to make examining more reliable. In the pursuit of reliable examining, all item banks so far constructed have limited themselves to multiple-choice or other thoroughly objective single mark items. But the essential point is only that the marking key leave no latitude for different markers to award different marks for the same answer—that is, completely reliable marking. Several groups are exploring the problems of banking 'structured' questions where several marks may be awarded to one question, in accordance with a strict marking key. There is also no reason why non-written questions—*e.g.* oral questions or performance tasks—should not be included in a bank. Indeed, the British Ability Scales (Elliot *et al.*, 1977) have shown that this can be done; the items on most of its sub-scales have been shown to fit the Rasch model, even when the stimulus mode is visual and the response mode motor or oral.

Tests and Examinations. Item banks are used to construct tests. It will be argued later that test characteristics can be predicted from item characteristics only if the bank, and hence the test, is calibrated on a single ability scale. An examiner may wish to assess candidates on more than one trait, but use of a bank will require him to consider only one trait at a time. This point will be taken up again later.

Item Banks and Item Pools. Choppin (1978) has proposed a useful distinction between two kinds of question collections. An *Item Pool* is a collection of items intended mainly to convey ideas to or stimulate the imagination of teachers and examiners in different institutions. Such pools have been in existence for many years, and range from informal collections generated by one or two school departments, through item pools organised by LEA's or Colleges of Education, to national examples like the NFER Biology Item Bank (Duckworth and Hoste, 1975) or the university and polytechnic Physics Item Bank set up at the Institute for Educational Technology, University of Surrey (Chelu and Elton, 1977), a co-operative enterprise supported by more than thirty tertiary institutions.

An *Item Bank* on the other hand is a measurement system. It consists of an adequate item pool together with the statistical and other information which enables tests to be constructed whose psychometric properties can be predicted in advance. The requirements for an item bank then are:

1. an adequate pool of items;

2. a 'catalogue' indicating the abilities and content being tested by each item;

3. statistical data from the behaviour of each item in calibration trials, and

4. a theory enabling the meaning of all scores on any test which may be constructed from the bank items to be defined in advance from the obtained item data.

In practice the distinction between pools and banks is not so clear. There is a whole spectrum of question collections meeting these requirements to different degrees. For example, the New Zealand Item Bank—Mathematics (New Zealand, 1973) contains some items (requirement 1) each linked to a specific behavioural objective, and catalogued accordingly (requirement 2). Each item is given 1, 2, 3 or 4 stars to indicate its difficulty as determined by extensive but unco-ordinated pre-testing. A test made up from this bank will provide useful information on the success of a course of teaching in attaining its objectives, and on the rank order of ability of the candidates taking it. But the statistical data given is not precise enough to ensure that two apparently similar tests are in fact of comparable difficulty (requirement 3) nor is there any way of predicting the variance of candidates' test scores, or even of ensuring that any particular segment of the ability range is adequately tested (requirement 4). Some other banks (*e.g.* Computerised Item Bank System (Newbould and Massey, 1977) which is used to produce some GCE objective tests) provide more precise facility values for their items, but in the absence of a satisfactory theory for predicting the distribution of test scores, the fourth requirement of a full measurement system is still missing. Much recent psychometric research has addressed this problem of predicting test parameters from item data.

Note: in order to include some important projects in this paper, it will be necessary at times to relax the fourth requirement and admit some 'item pools' which Choppin would not admit as 'item banks'.

C

2. Measurement with an Item Bank

It is normal in psychological and statistical research for advances to be made first of all within narrow and somewhat unreal restrictions. At present the enormous potential of item banking can be realised only under the assumption already referred to, that a test is required to measure accurately a single trait. Once this fundamental problem of measurement is solved, it may prove possible to apply the solution in a wider context.

Unidimensional Test Theory. It has always been at least an implicit assumption in test construction that one single trait is being measured. Even if items are included which are supposed to sample different mental skills, the final selection of items is made largely on the basis of the discrimination index or item/test point-biserial correlation coefficient, each of which estimates the extent to which one item measures the same 'thing' as the total test score: whatever that 'thing' is, it is a single 'thing'.

In recent years, several 'latent trait models' of test performance have been proposed. These assume that there exists a single scale on which all the items can be placed, ordered according to their difficulty, and that this order is fixed for all persons attempting the items. Furthermore, all the candidates can be placed on this scale, ordered according to their ability, and this order is independent of the actual items attempted. There is thus a single scale (measuring the latent trait) which measures (is) both difficulty and ability simultaneously. An analogy may be drawn with weighing people using a balance or see-saw: certain standard objects may be ordered according to their weights (difficulty of being lifted) and people may be tried against them, and ordered according to their weights (abilities to raise the weights). Both orders will be unique—whether the weighting is done on Earth or on the Moon.

The simplest theoretical model for such a scale is that of Guttman (1950). A Guttman scale consists of items (and people) such that when a person encounters an item below his ability he *always* gets it right, while he *always* gets wrong any item above his ability. There is no room for error, or chance; however narrow the ability/difficulty gap, the outcome is determined. Unfortunately this model requires items which discriminate perfectly at one point on the scale, and also perfectly consistent behaviour from the candidates. In practice neither requirement seems achievable or even approachable; no matter how carefully a test is constructed some (indeed most) candidates will be right on a few items apparently more difficult than ones they are wrong on. A probabilistic, rather than deterministic, model is needed to account for this uncertainty.

A Rasch scale (Rasch, 1960; Wright, 1977) is essentially a probabilistic Guttman scale. In this model, when a person encounters an item whose difficulty (d) is below his ability (a) he is expected to get it right, and the greater the gap (a–d) the more confident we are in expecting him to get it right. With an item exactly at his ability level, when $(a - d) = 0$, he is given a 50–50 chance of success (the Guttman model is unable to predict anything in this most interesting case). This is written mathematically as:

$$\Pr (X = 0 \text{ or } 1) = \frac{\exp X(a - d)}{1 + \exp (a - d)}$$

The probability of a wrong answer ($X = 0$) or a right answer ($X = 1$) by a person on an item is a function of the difference between his ability and its difficulty. (The particular function used is simply a convenient one to translate the $(a - d)$ range, $-\infty$ to $+\infty$, into the range 0 to 1.) Similar equations can be written for all the items one person takes, inserting the appropriate d's and X's, and then the person's ability is estimated as the value of 'a' in these equations which gives the biggest joint probability for them—the value of 'a' which is most likely to result in this particular set of right and wrong answers. In a similar way, by comparing the equations for all persons in a sample on one item, the difficulty of that item can be estimated as the maximum likelihood value of 'd'. This estimation is easily carried out by computer, and an approximation easily handled with a pocket calculator is described by Wright (1977). Once the test is calibrated, of course, such calculations are no longer necessary.

The Rasch model involves just these two parameters—item difficulty and person ability—both of which can be located on a single scale. More complicated models have been proposed, such as those by Birnbaum (1968) and Lord (1952) which involve one or two extra parameters. The addition of an 'item discriminating power' and an 'item guessability' parameter do allow latent trait models to fit real data more closely, but to allow for the estimation of the extra parameters more data is needed: setting up an item bank using the three item parameter model would involve trying out every item on at least 2,000 persons, compared to the 2–300 needed for estimation of the Rasch parameters.

There are more profound objections than this. If an item parameter for 'guessability' is necessary, then is a corresponding person parameter for 'guessing ability' not equally necessary? And should there not also be a 'person discriminating power', estimating the extent to which a person is being measured on the same trait as the rest of the sample? Logic seems to demand item/person symmetry when the only data we have comes from item/person interaction.

A particular comment should be made about item discrimination indices, a standard feature of classical item analysis. While the Guttman scale requires all items to discriminate perfectly and the Rasch scale requires that they all discriminate equally, the Birnbaum and Lord scales allow discrimination to vary. But consider how 2 items, A of high and B of low discrimination, but of similar difficulty, compare for different ability groups. In a high ability group nearly everyone would get A right, but only a majority get B right; hence A is easier than B. In a low ability group hardly anyone would get A right while several get B right; here B is easier than A (see diagram).

Which item is really the easier? The question cannot be answered. The items cannot be ordered uniquely on the difficulty scale; their relative difficulty depends on the people used to compare them. It is to avoid this conceptual and practical difficulty that the restriction of equal discrimination is imposed. Items A and C discriminate equally. Their curves are parallel, and never cross.

The final advantage of the Rasch model over the other latent trait ones is that it is in fact the model implicitly assumed by anyone who uses a candidate's total score on a test as the measure of his ability, as most of us do. Whenever a test is used to provide a single score for each person, unidimensionality is implicitly assumed; and

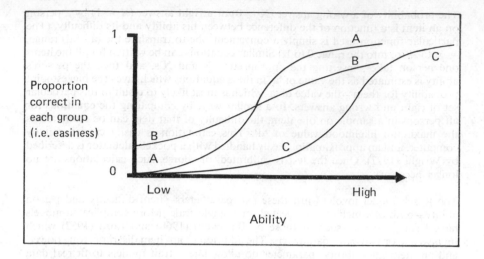

whenever this score is simply the number of items correct, equal discrimination and hence the Rasch model are similarly assumed. (For a proof of this, see Andersen (1977).) Even if a more complex model where items are differentially weighted according to their discriminating power and guessability comes to be used in test standardisation, the simplicity of the Rasch model is likely to prove indispensable in item banking.

The Rasch model has been shown to fit adequately to real test data of many kinds, even though the tests were not constructed in accordance with its assumptions. It does not work well if:

a. the test is highly speeded—the model assumes that everyone gets a fair chance at every item;

b. the test is essentially one of knowledge—there is no dimension on which to place the items uniquely;

c. the test confounds two or more poorly correlated dimensions.

Obviously the applicability of the model will be improved if only items that conform to the 'equal discrimination' are allowed into the test or bank. In practice, such is the robustness of the model when more than 20 or so items are used in a test, that most items that would pass the traditional item selection criteria will be accepted by the Rasch model—the word 'equal' can be interpreted fairly loosely.

In summary, the Rasch approach seems a useful, practicable way of obtaining measures of person abilities and, since these measures do not depend on the particular set of items taken, seems to be particularly suitable for item banking.

3. Constructing Tests from Item Banks

Early item 'banks' (or pools) were collections of items usually written for school certificate or degree examinations, and it was common practice to record the classical facility value (percentage correct) obtained each time the item was used. These of course varied from sample to sample, and an examination constructor had to guess, with the help of experience, the facility value he might expect from his own group.

If facility values could be collected from nationally representative random samples then much of this uncertainty would be removed—a teacher who knew (roughly) his group's relative standing could be sure of obtaining a test of the right level and spread of difficulty. But this procedure would be similar to the standardisation of a new test—an expensive and difficult job for 50 or 100 items, and quite impracticable for several thousand. A compromise has been used by some banks; the ACER Science Item Bank (ACER, 1978) used state-wide samples of about 300, and difficulty levels are reported on a five point scale. Scores on different tests constructed from this bank cannot be compared—the tests provide only rank orders with no norm or criterion-reference—but the teacher is at least assured of an appropriate test.

But however accurate the statistics are, a bank based on classical item analysis cannot provide a true measurement system, for while the average difficulty of the test can be fairly accurately predicted (assuming that the items operate independently) the eventual spread of scores cannot. Swineford (1974) has developed an empirical multiple regression formula to predict the raw score standard deviation using as predictors functions of the average item-test biserial correlation and of the mean and spread of item difficulties (expressed as normal curve deviates). But for several reasons, not least of which is the desire to escape the normal distribution assumptions, such formulae have found little application in item banking.

Only latent trait models can permit *all* scores (not just the 50th percentile) to be translated into estimates of ability on a common scale. In the Rasch model all item trait-biserials are equal, and only the mean and spread of item difficulties are needed. An approximation to the exact procedure can be written

$$b_t = M + X \ln \left(\frac{t}{L - t} \right)$$

where b_t is the ability estimate for a raw score t,
M is the mean difficulty,
X is a function of item difficulty variance, and
L is the test length.

When a test is constructed from the bank, a table giving b_t for every value of raw score can be easily produced; that is, a conversion table can be prepared in advance. (Wright and Stone, 1978.)

This leads to the most important advantage of a Rasch-scaled item bank: all tests made up from it are automatically equated. Since a person's score on any test can be converted into an ability estimate on the common bank scale, any group of people can be given a test made up of items particularly suitable for them, yet all the results can be compared with each other.

Domain, Criterion and Norm-Referenced Testing. An item bank is merely a calibrated set of items; it is thus neutral with respect to the referencing controversy. It will nonetheless be useful to see how an item bank would be used to provide several kinds of test.

Domain-Referenced:

In this kind of testing we are interested in inferring student achievement over the whole domain rather than in knowledge of achievement on the particular test. Shoemaker (1976) argues that 'we must have the capability of generating a large number of randomly parallel tests for each subdomain of interest'. This necessarily requires an item bank, or item domain 'constructed such that, for all practical purposes performance on the item domain is equivalent to performance on the item universe', the set of all possible items which 'may be used to assess mastery on that skill'. Although Shoemaker's interest is more in course evaluation than in student evaluation, clearly an item bank is a prerequisite of any domain-referenced testing.

Criterion-Referenced:

Much so-called criterion-referenced testing would be better described as domain referenced, and as such is covered by the previous comments. When a test is to be used to decide whether candidates have reached a required criterion level, either to proceed to the next part of the course, or to be awarded a pass certificate, then a different test construction procedure may be appropriate. If the items in a certain domain can be ranged along a difficulty dimension, then a point on that dimension can be identified as a cut-off point; successful candidates can cope with most of the items below that point, while unsuccessful ones cannot cope with most items above that point. The most efficient test (the shortest test that adequately divides the two groups) will consist only of items with difficulties at or close to the cut-off point. Once the acceptable error level is decided, the required standard error of measurement and hence the required test length can be calculated, and that number of items is selected from the bank as close as possible to the criterion level. While this can be done using facility values for a reasonably stable group of candidates, wider application to varied groups and with various criterion levels will be much easier using the Rasch indices—in effect, the criterion is calibrated onto the scale just like another item. The procedure can of course easily be generalised to several criterion levels to facilitate the awarding of grades.

Norm-Referenced:

Just as rulers and weighing machines functioned well enough to describe people as soon as a scale was agreed, so a calibrated item bank will be of immediate use to testers and teachers. But just as doctors and insurance companies find normative data of value, so will a calibrated item bank become more and more useful as such data are gathered. It will be possible for national monitoring exercises to gather data for precise norm description, but this will be additional, rather than essential, to the bank's use as a measuring instrument. The scale itself, like the standard metre bar in Paris, will be constant from year to year; experience will soon show testers what levels of performance to expect from particular groups. Given such information, any score from the bank will automatically be norm-referenced, if the tester wishes to consider it in this way. If a latent-trait approach is adopted, only an initial set of items need be normed on a nationally representative sample; later items can be added on by administering them with some of the initial set to any convenient sample. It is intended that the British Ability Scales may grow in this way (Elliott *et al.*, 1977).

Best Test Design:

If an item bank is considered as a measuring instrument, then a 'best test' can be defined as one which minimises the standard errors of measurement over the whole range of persons measured. (This assumes that no specific criterion level has been chosen for maximum discrimination.) Wright and Douglas (1975) have shown that this is achieved better in most circumstances, and almost as well in others, by a test in which the item difficulties are uniformly, rather than normally, distributed. This is in accordance with traditional test construction practice, in which item distribution is always more uniform than sample distribution. Simple efficient rules are given by Wright for generating a 'best test' from a Rasch calibrated bank, and for preparing the conversion table in advance, so that scripts can be marked and ability measures obtained immediately after the test is completed.

4. Applications

Item banks are finding applications throughout the education system, from primary school to university. In this section some examples are given of banks which have been or are being constructed for the following applications:
Examinations
Monitoring Standards
Classroom Assessment
Diagnosis
Local Research

Examinations. Many school examining boards (including SCEEB) have, since the introduction of objective testing, retained the items for future re-use. There are several advantages:

a.   some at least of the labour of writing and pre-testing new items is saved;

b.   the difficulty level of the re-used items is accurately known, and the standard of the test can be more reliably maintained;

c.   if these items prove to be more or less difficult than before, this is direct evidence for some change in the standard of teaching or learning on that part of the syllabus.

Many university and college departments are building up their own item banks for similar reasons. Most notable in tertiary education have been medical departments, such as Middlesex Hospital Medical School and Edinburgh University Department of Medical Bacteriology, where multiple-choice tests have since the sixties been used in all of the five or six years of training.

More recently examination banks have been expanded from this local level and made available to several examining bodies at once. The Scottish universities, for example, share a bank of questions (with facility values) for examining in the first two years of Chemistry courses. A potential benefit is the chance to compare standards between different boards or colleges before the examination is taken, thus doing away with the need for any *post-hoc* comparability study. The Royal College of Physicians have since 1969 drawn from a bank of 8,000 items for the first (and only written) paper in their Part II examination, thus ensuring equivalence between their three institutions. But a Rasch-based bank would allow different institutions to construct different tests, yet still award equivalent grades. The implication for school-based examining is clear; the Biology Item Bank (Duckworth and Hoste, 1976) can be seen as a first step towards an item bank system designed to facilitate internal assessment as part of school certificate examining. It must be pointed out that Rasch-calibrated item banks will only provide measures of *ability* in a subject, or of the several distinct *abilities* involved in the subject. If an assessment of breadth of *knowledge* is also required (and this seems to be involved as much as ability in most examinations) a separate approach, perhaps using a domain-referenced bank, will also be necessary. Such a two-pronged attack, on breadth of knowledge and depth of understanding, seems to have much to commend it.

Monitoring. The Assessment of Performance Unit of the DES in England (APU) began its monitoring programme in autumn 1978 with a survey of mathematical achievement in schools in England and Wales. An earlier DES sponsored project, Tests of Attainment in Mathematics in Schools (Sumner, 1975, 1977), had developed two item banks, for 11- and 15-year-olds, and these were used to produce the written monitoring tests. Collections of practical maths 'items' were also developed, but not calibrated. Item banks will also be used in 'scientific development' surveys, and perhaps in some of the other areas. Use of the Rasch model in the interpretation of the surveys will allow relative changes in difficulty of specific items or content areas over the years to be more accurately monitored.

It is intended that the monitoring study results will be reported in two forms (APU, 1978). First, a global measure will be given; this implies that all of the items will be considered as measuring one trait—unidimensional measurement. But, using the Rasch approach, various combinations of items will also be used to generate measures of sub-skills, either in different content areas or of different, psychologically significant, abilities. The result will be a profile of standards in whatever distinct psychological or educational abilities are identified.

Classroom Assessment. Books of test questions or 'revision exercises' have always been popular with teachers, but have always been criticised, both as teaching aids and tests, for their possible influence on teaching practice and because they offer no interpretative framework or psychometric reference. Recent enthusiasm for 'criterion-referenced' tests has encouraged some publishers to produce books of items grouped under teaching objectives, and thereby, with no indication even of the difficulty levels of the items, to claim to be providing a reference system.

Clearly there is a need for good (pedagogically and psychometrically) test material for teachers which allows them to monitor

a.   the effectiveness of their teaching, and

b.   the efficiency of each pupil's learning.

Such material needs to be appropriate to the syllabus and style of each and every teacher, and simultaneously to refer scores to some measurement frame. Item banks seem best able to offer such flexibility.

Most work so far has been done in Australia, New Zealand or the USA. Tasmania (Palmer, 1974) has a Primary Social Sciences bank designed to provide the teacher with feedback on class achievement. The tests are constructed by the teacher, but marked and interpreted centrally. The New Zealand Item Bank: Mathematics, which ranges over six years of primary and early secondary school, and the Australian Item Banks in Mathematics, Science and Social Science, mainly aimed at 'Year 10', (ACER, 1978) are wholly school based. Each of these banks consists of a published book (or books) containing all of the items on detachable pages. The teacher is required to choose items, photocopy the pages, cut out the items, and paste up and duplicate the test. Item difficulty is indicated on a four or five point scale, allowing rough control over test difficulty, but having no reference to normative or other data.

One fully operational item bank system for school use has been designed to reduce the amount of work required of the teachers. The Portland Public School system in Oregon, USA, has produced Rasch-calibrated item banks in mathematics, reading and language arts (Forster et al., 1978). Teachers request tests for various purposes by specifying the required test characteristics (see Best Test Design) and receive the test, either a master copy or multiple copies, within a week, together with reference and semi-diagnostic information.

Two major projects under way in Britain aim to develop systems like the Portland one. In England, the LEAs' and Schools' Item Bank Project (NFER, 1978) is producing banks of language and mathematics items (written by the project team) for ages 7–15; in Scotland the Primary Mathematics Item Bank Project (Pollitt, 1978) is creating a bank of teacher-written maths items for ages 7–12. Both projects are using the Rasch approach to develop an objective measurement system such that teachers (and LEAs, especially in the (LEASIB project) can specify the test they need by referring to a catalogue of 'objectives of teaching', and obtain, along with the test, a conversion table giving measures on the standard national scale. It is hoped that some other Scottish projects, notably the Assessment of Early Mathematics (Duncan, 1978) and the Item Bank project at Moray House College of Education which will develop items for pupils of lower ability in S3–S4 mathematics, will also be linked to this scale. Indeed, a single UK mathematics achievement scale from 7–18 seems likely to be established in the near future.

A final point is that item banks are never complete—there is always room for growth. New items can, and must, be added as the curriculum develops, and teachers should be encouraged to criticise the items in the bank and to submit new ones. New items are easily calibrated by being included in a test with established items. The whole enterprise should encourage a healthy reappraisal of one's teaching.

Diagnosis. Perhaps the principal advantage of item banks in diagnosis is that they allow the tester to define the ability or content area of interest for himself. By treating the test as a set of sub-tests, a profile can be obtained which should be more meaningful to the teacher than one derived from a published test. Furthermore, any particular sub-test can be extended by adding items to increase the precision of measurement for each individual.

For a more detailed diagnosis of the causes of failure in individuals, item banks are not enough. But they do provide large pools of proven items in which a teaching

C*

expert can look for items with good diagnostic properties. It is to be hoped that such tests will be developed in the near future.

Local Research. A perennial dilemma for anyone wishing to assess attainment in a research project is whether to use a standardised test which gives generalisable measures, but will never be quite appropriate to his samples, or to spend time and funds developing his own thoroughly appropriate instruments, whose results cannot be interpreted generally (Wilmott, 1976). A particularly intractable problem involves the comparison of different courses with different teaching styles—no common test can be fair to both groups.

A Rasch item bank will often provide the answer. Any selection of items will provide scores interpretable on the standard scale (so long, of course, as all the children have been adequately exposed to the style and material in them). Thus local results can be interpreted in a national context. When a new course is designed, it may be necessary to write new items for it and to calibrate these onto the bank by combining them in one test with some established items.

5. Summary

This paper has described some of the important work that has been or is being done in an attempt to realise the enormous potential of item banking, and has outlined some of the hoped for benefits. It must be admitted that some of these ideas, especially those involving use of the Rasch model in monitoring and diagnosis, are as yet unproven. Wood and Skurnik, in their seminal study of the subject in 1969, said:

'Item banking is an examining technique for the future'.

Nine years later, the future is beginning to turn into the present.

References

Andersen, E. B. (1977). 'Sufficient statistics and latent trait models'. *Psychometrika, 42* (1), 69–81.

APU (1978). *Monitoring Mathematics*. Dept. of Educ. and Science, London.

ACER (1978). *Mathematics Item Bank*. Books 1 and 2 and Teachers Handbook. *Science Item Bank*, Books 1, 2 and 3. *Science Item Bank Handbook. Social Science Item Bank* (and Item Bank Handbook). Australian Council for Educational Research; Hawthorn, Vic.

Birnbaum, A. (1968). 'Some Latent Trait Models' in *Statistical Theories of Mental Test Scores*. Lord and Novick, Addison-Wesley; Reading, Mass.

Chelu, C. J. and Elton, L. R. B. (1977). 'An item bank for multiple-choice questions'. *Physics Education*, May 1977.

Choppin, B. (1978). 'Item Banking and the Monitoring of Achievement'. *Research in Progress* No. 1. NFER; Slough, Berks.

Duckworth, D. and Hoste, H. R. (1976). *Question Banking: Approach through Biology*. Schools Council Examinations Bulletin 35, Evans/Methuen.

Duncan, A. P. (1978). *Assessment of Early Mathematics*. Mathematics Dept., Hamilton College of Education, Lanarkshire.

Elliott, C. D., Murray, D. J. and Pearson, L. S. (1977). *The British Ability Scales*. NFER; Slough, Berks.

Forster, F. and Doherty, V. (1978). *Using the Rasch approach to measurement to solve practical school testing problems.*

Forster, F., Ascher, G. and Carr, C. (1978). *Research on the Rasch measurement model*. Papers read at the Convention of the American Educational Research Association, Toronto.

Guttman, L. (1950). 'The basis for scalogram analysis' in *Studies in Social Psychology in World War II*. Stoufer, S. *et al*. Princeton U.P., Princeton N.J.

Lord, F. M. (1952). *A theory of test scores*. Psychometrica Monograph, 1–84.

Newbould, C. A. and Massey, A. J. (1977). 'A computerised item banking system'. *Br. J. Educ. Tech., 8* (2), 114–123.

New Zealand (1973). *Item Bank: Mathematics Level 2 and Level 6*. New Zealand, Dept. of Education, Wellington.

NFER (1978). *LEAs' and Schools' Item Bank Project. General Brochure*. National Foundation for Educational Research, Slough, Berks.

Palmer, D. G. (1974). *A Computerised Self-Moderation Procedure in Banks of Items for Primary Social Sciences*. Curriculum Centre, Education Dept. of Tasmania.

Pollitt, A. B. (1978). *Item Banking in Primary Mathematics*. Godfrey Thomson Unit, University of Edinburgh.

Rasch, G. (1960). *Probabilistic Models for some Intelligence and Attainment Tests*. Danish Institute for Educational Research.

Shoemaker, D. M. (1976). 'Applicability of item banking and matrix sampling to educational assessment' in *Advances in Psychological and Educational Measurement*. de Gruijter, D. N. M. and van der Kamp, L. J. T. Wiley, London.

Sumner, R. (1975). *Tests of Attainment in Mathematics in School: Monitoring Feasibility Study.* (1977). *Tests of Attainment in Mathematics in School: Continuation of Monitoring Feasibility Study.* NFER, Windsor.

Swineford, F. (1974). *The test-maker's problem of predicting the score standard deviation*. Educational Testing Service, Princeton, N.J.

Willmott, A. S. (1976). 'The place of item banks in local research'. *Research Intelligence, 2*, (2).

Wood, R. and Skurnik, L. S. (1969). *Item Banking*. NFER, Slough.

Wright, B. D. (1977). 'Solving Measurement Problems with the Rasch Model'. *J. Educ. Meas., 14*, (2), 97–116.

Wright, B. D. and Douglas, G. A (1975). *Best Test Design and Self-Tailored Testing*. Research Memorandum 19, Stat Laboratory, Dept. of Educ. University of Chicago.

Wright, B. D. and Stone, M .H. (1978). *Best Test Design: A Handbook for Rasch Measurement*. Scientific Press.

THE STANDARDISATION OF SCHOOL ASSESSMENT

If, as Munn and Dunning propose, there are to be differentiated syllabuses and certification at different levels, allied to a measure of internal assessment then two problems immediately arise. One is concerned with moderation of syllabuses, assessment instruments and marking schemes, the other with standardisation. Two aspects of standardisation have to be considered, the one general—and it was raised in the introduction to the last paper—the other is more particular and concerns the problem of using statistical techniques when small groups of candidates are involved. At present the SCEEB has very many such groups presented for 'O' grade; the number will be dramatically increased if we ever have certification for all in the form which Dunning recommends.

Dr David Walker was, until he retired, Director of the Scottish Council for Research in Education and ten years on he is still as active as ever. He was part author, some seventeen years ago, of a book on the problems of scaling in which the problem of scaling small groups was addressed. In this paper he describes the possible processes and examines their likely effectiveness. His conclusions are reassuring. He was involved in a study of the same problem in small group scaling for the Munn/Dunning feasibility studies and makes use of some of his findings in this paper.

A.W.J.

The Standardisation of School Assessment

D. A. Walker

The Need for Standardisation

One of the main recommendations of the Dunning Report is that assessments provided by the school should form an integral part of the measures on which certificates are awarded at the end of the fourth year of secondary education in Scottish schools (*Dunning*, §8.12). From the evidence given to the Committee it would appear that teachers are generally in favour of such a change, although some have reservations founded on staffing difficulties or lack of expertise (*Dunning*, §5.52).

Most teachers, while confident of their ability to assess the achievements of their pupils in relation to those of their classmates, and probably in relation to those of pupils taught in previous years, are hesitant about their ability to relate those achievements to those of pupils in other schools or to the achievements of the whole group of pupils being presented for examination at the end of the fourth year (*Dunning*, §5.60). This hesitation is well founded, since teachers do not normally have the information which would enable them to make these judgements, apart from their knowledge of the grades awarded to their pupils in former years.

Evidence of how much variation there is between schools in the ability to produce comparable estimates is rather scarce, but the Scottish Certificate in Education Examination Board carried out an investigation in 1974 and found that internal assessments tended generally to underestimate performance (*Dunning:* Appendix V, §7). Similar findings were obtained in a research project conducted by the Scottish Council for Research in Education (*Dunning:* Appendix V, §8). In both cases there were instances of wide discrepancies between internal assessments and performance in the external examination. Internal assessments therefore require standardisation before the data from different schools can be regarded as comparable.

Methods of Standardisation

The term 'standardisation' has slightly different meanings in different educational contexts and it is therefore necessary to state that in this article it refers to the processes by which the internal assessments provided by the school, for pupils being presented in a given subject, are transformed to make them comparable between schools. The more complicated and debatable question of making them comparable between subjects, such as English and Modern Studies, is not included in this discussion.

There are two main features of a school's set of assessments which normally require attention. The first is the average of the set; has the school underestimated or overestimated the average achievement of the group of pupils? A correction for this can easily be applied by the addition or subtraction of the required amount to or from each pupil's assessment. The second feature is the scatter or spread of the assessments; has the school bunched its measures too closely or has it spread them over too wide a range? The correction here, though slightly more complicated, is arithmetically simple and ensures that pupils well above or well below the average are given justice.

Normally, standardisation does not interfere with the order of merit supplied by the school. Some standardisation processes also preserve the relative spacing of the assessments; if the school is of the opinion that the gap between pupil A and pupil B is greater than that between pupil B and pupil C the relationship can be preserved. On the other hand, assessments which are given in the form of a rank order of pupils do not provide information about the relative sizes of these gaps, and assumptions about them must be made in the process of standardisation.

There are three main methods which can be used to standardise internal assessments, and the rest of this article is devoted to a discussion of their advantages and disadvantages and of the assumptions which underlie each. The order in which they are given is one of convenience and not necessarily of merit. They are (a) moderation, (b) using item banks, and (c) scaling.

Moderation

'Moderation' is another term which has different connotations for different writers. In a 1972 publication of the New Zealand Council for Educational Research (Elley and Livingstone, 1972), it is defined as 'any method of determining the differences in attainment of various groups of pupils' and is therefore a synonym for standardisation. A similar nomenclature is used in the *Schools Council Examinations Bulletin 37* (1977), where three methods of moderation are defined as (a) moderation by inspection, (b) statistical moderation, and (c) consortium moderation. The report of the Scottish Certificate of Education Examinations Board on the assessment of practical work in Science (1978, §28), also uses the term 'statistical moderation'. In the present article the term is restricted, as in the Dunning Report (*Dunning*, §2.16; 4.15; 7.10), to one type of standardisation, the essence of which is that the work of a sample of the pupils in a school is examined by a person or team of persons (the moderators) from outside the school, with a view to determining what changes are required in the assessments of these pupils, and hence in those of their schoolmates, to bring them into line with the external standards as framed by the moderators.

The methods adopted in applying the principle vary widely. The moderators may be inspectors or teachers from other schools; they require and are usually given some training in the necessary techniques; they may examine work submitted to a central point or may spend some time in the school; some may be released from their duties as teachers while undertaking the task of moderation. Moderation by inspection is already used in Scotland for oral and practical tests and for the assessment of project work. The Dunning Report considers that it probably gives a better guarantee than the scaling process that the syllabus has been covered (*Dunning*, §7.11). Consortium moderation occurs where teachers from a group of schools meet and agree on standards of performance expected at each level.

Some of the assumptions underlying the idea of moderation are the following:

1. Teachers are able to determine the relative achievements of their own pupils with reasonable validity and reliability; *i.e.* moderation is required only for a sample.

2. Moderators have reasonably stable standards against which they can evaluate the work of a wide range of pupils.

3. Sufficient time is available for moderators to carry out their tasks during the final stage of the fourth year, *i.e.* no school is judged on standards reached some time before the end of the course.

The process of moderation may also be used to adjust the syllabus in schools participating in an area or national scheme, but this is a different context and lies outwith the field considered in this article.

One advantage of moderation is that it almost certainly increases the number of contacts between teachers in different schools, and this is appreciated by some teachers. The training in, and further insight into, the techniques of assessment and moderation are also beneficial. Among the disadvantages are the difficulties of selecting appropriate samples for examination, the time-consuming nature of the operation, the dependence on the skill of the moderators, and the cost. Some of these schemes can be very elaborate. It is not clear whether the reference in the Dunning Report to moderation processes being regarded as burdensome by many teachers (in Queensland) applies to moderation of syllabuses or assessments or both (*Dunning*, §6.27).

Item Banks

A second method of standardisation depends more on assisting teachers to standardise their own assessments than on rectifying assessments already submitted. It assumes the existence of a bank of items which have already been applied to a sufficiently large and representative sample of pupils at the appropriate stage to enable their difficulty levels to be reliably assessed. It also assumes that this bank is available to teachers, who can select an adequate number of items, apply them to their classes, and so determine for each pupil the appropriate internal assessment.

Advantages of this method are that teachers have access to a wide range of items, and probably spend much less time in preparing examinations. There are, however, many difficulties to be overcome before that stage is reached. The preparation and maintenance of item banks in the various subjects would be a major operation. If there are changes in emphasis on topics in curricula, difficulty levels of items are bound to vary from time to time. Some subjects, for example English Literature, do not lend themselves readily to the construction of suitable items. Most teachers would require inservice training in the methods of applying the techniques.

The main assumptions underlying the method are (a) that the preparation and maintenance of item banks are feasible; (b) that teachers in schools would be able, with the assistance of data obtained by the application of tests constructed from items from the bank, to construct reliable assessments for their pupils. It is obvious that a great deal of research and development is required before this approach can be generally useful, and it is good to know that at least one research project on item banking is already under way in Scotland. This is taking place at the Godfrey Thomson Unit, University of Edinburgh.

Scaling

The third method depends on the existence and use of scores made by the pupils concerned in an external examination common to all the pupils for whom the internal assessments have to be standardised. The average of the internal assessments provided by the school for the pupils presented for a given subject is adjusted to become equal to the average of the scores made by these pupils in the external examination in that subject. The spread or scatter of the internal assessments is adjusted to equal the scatter of the scores made by the pupils in the external examination. These processes do not change the order of merit within the school group, which remains that provided by the school.

There are several methods of making these adjustments, but this discussion is confined to one which may be described as linear scaling and is represented diagrammatically in Figure 1. It uses data from a school presenting candidates for the O-grade examination in English in 1977. Each cross indicates a pupil's scores in the school's assessment and in the external examination. The straight line used for scaling is drawn through the point representing the average score of the school group in internal and external assessments, and its slope is determined by the scatters of the two sets of marks. The fact that the external and internal assessments both averaged nearly 50 in this group is a peculiarity of the data from this group and not a general principle. The internal assessment 43 is scaled by following the lines AB, BC to produce the scaled assessment 46; internal assessment 64 becomes scaled assessment 59, and so on. The same results are obtained by straightforward arithmetic. The scaled assessments thus assume two of the characteristics of the external examination; if that examination has been a national one, the scaled assessments have a national relevance.

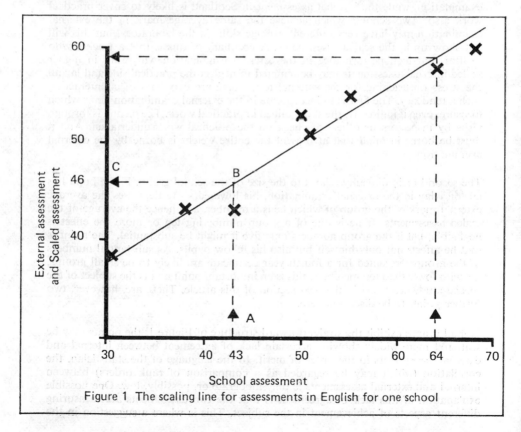

Figure 1 The scaling line for assessments in English for one school

75

The main assumptions underlying this method are:

1. that the external examination gives a valid and reliable estimate of the average and scatter of the school group's achievements;

2. that the school has given a reliable assessment of the order of merit in English and of the relative spacing of the pupils;

3. that the relation between internal and external assessments is sufficiently strong to justify scaling the first on the second.

The advantages of the method are (a) that it provides a simple and easily justifiable way of standardising the internal assessments, and (b) that it throws no extra burden on the teacher, as the scaling operation is conducted centrally, and would on a national scale probably be carried out by a computer. The disadvantages warrant more detailed discussion.

The first is that the third assumption may not be well-founded. For example, an external examination in science on a national scale is almost certain to be a written examination, while the internal assessment in Scotland is likely to cover practical work also. Two schools which achieve the same average mark in the external examination may have very different average skills in the laboratory, but this will not show up in the scaled assessments. A corollary of this is that a teacher who realises that high performance in the external examination will result in higher scaled internal assessments may be tempted to neglect the practical side and lay all the stress on teaching for the external test. There are two ways of counteracting such a tendency. The first is to incorporate in the external examination items which measure, even if indirectly, the skills gained in practical work. The second is through visits by inspectors or others to check on the practical work undertaken. And it must be borne in mind that at present the entire weight is borne by the external examination.

The second main difficulty relates to the size of the school group. If one pupil has an 'off' day in the external examination, his lowered score depresses the average external mark of the group of which he is a member, and hence the average of the scaled assessments. If he is one of a group numbering ten or more the effect is negligible, but if the group numbers only five it might be substantial. The point is that he affects not only himself but also his fellow pupils. As substantial numbers of the groups presented for a fourth year certificate are likely to be small groups, *i.e.* with fewer than ten members, this is an important point and is the subject of the special study described in the next section of this article. There are, however, two further points to be discussed here.

Not all graphs exhibit the straightforward structure of Figure 1, the points may be scattered more widely showing a certain lack of agreement between internal and external assessments in the order of merit. In the language of the statistician, the correlation (which may be regarded as a comparison of rank orders) between internal and external assessments is only moderate or, possibly, low. One possible explanation of this lack of agreement is that the two assessments are measuring different aspects of achievement in the subject. This is where a suggestion in the

Dunning Report—that provision be made for a more general moderation of the work of a sample of schools—is a valuable one (*Dunning*, §8.13). The constraints of time might mean that this moderation was conducted after the issue of the certificates, but it would throw light on the reasons for the discrepancies between the two sets of assessments and possibly prevent their recurrence.

The size of the correlation coefficient is not the sole factor to be considered when groups are small. In these groups there is a greater chance of the pupils forming a fairly homogeneous group; it is then difficult for either the school or the external examination to produce a reliable order of merit, and the correlation may be low. Nevertheless there may be a clear relation between the two groups of assessments and the school group may be eminently scaleable. For example, five pupils presented by a school may have been given internal assessments 61, 62, 63, 64, 65, and then receive external assessments 63, 61, 65, 62, 64. The correlation is relatively low ($r = 0.3$) but the average and scatter are both equivalent and the internal assessments can be accepted without change. A low correlation is therefore not a sufficient reason in some cases for rejecting internal assessments.

A Study of Small Groups

An analysis of the presentations for the O-grade Certificate in 1977 showed that a substantial proportion of the groups of pupils contained fewer than ten members. A group is here defined as all the candidates in a school who were presented for the examination in a particular subject. If the proposals of the Dunning Committee for Credit, General and Foundation levels are accepted, and if different examinations are set for these levels, the number of these small groups is likely to be even larger. With the co-operation of the Scottish Certificate of Education Examination Board a study was therefore conducted into the operation of scaling some of the small groups presented for the 1977 examinations.

The Board made available for the study the O-grade marks of a representative number of groups containing five to nine pupils. The sample was drawn from the whole of Scotland and covered presentations in Accounting, Art and Design, Biology, English, German, Home Economics, Latin, Mathematics, and Modern Studies. Almost all of the schools involved kindly supplied the school marks on which were based the ranks submitted to the Board; these marks were treated as the internal assessments. In all, there were 74 usable groups provided by 64 schools.

For each group a graph of the type shown in Figure 1 was constructed, the scaled assessments were calculated, and each graph was inspected for 'flop' scores, *i.e.*, cases where the performance of a pupil in the external examination was markedly below what would be expected from the school mark and the performance of the other members of the group. Note was also taken of what might be termed 'flash in the pan' scores, where the mark in the external examination was markedly higher than expected. The findings may be summarised thus:

1. There was a high level of agreement between the school marks and the O-grade marks. In terms of correlation coefficients, 31 of the 74 groups yielded correlations exceeding 0.9, and 43 had correlations exceeding 0.8. Only 10 had correlations between 0.5 and zero and one had a negative value;

2. Where subjects with practical aspects were concerned, the correlations were

still reasonably high. Of the 12 for Biology six exceeded 0·9; of the 10 for Home Economics five exceeded 0·8;

3.   There were only two clear cases of flop scores, one in English (seven pupils in the group) and one in Modern Studies (nine pupils in the group).

Since this investigation was completed the Examination Board has published its report on the assessment of practical work in Science subjects. In that investigation the smallest classes in which scaling was applied each contained four pupils, and no problems appear to have arisen (SCEEB Report, 1978).

It would therefore seem that there is little to fear from the effects of 'flop' scores at this stage. The technique which was devised and used for dealing with them at the stage of transfer from primary to secondary education (McIntosh, Walker and Mackay, 1962), when the pupils were about 12 years of age, appears to be unnecessary when the pupils have reached the age of 16. This is a comforting conclusion since the technique involved the scanning of graphs, the number of which might be overwhelming in a national examination situation.

For the same reasons it would appear that a second look is necessary at the statement in the Dunning Report that 'moderation by inspection on a sample basis will probably be an essential element . . . where small assessment groups occur' (§7.11). Further research, using a larger number of samples and new computer techniques, is required.

Further Comments and Conclusions

From the information which has been presented and discussed in the preceding sections we may conclude that there will be a place for each of the three methods of standardisation. The Dunning Report recommends that standardisation should mainly be achieved by scaling, as it is valid for the majority of subjects and more economical than moderation (*Dunning*, §8.13). Moderation procedures might have to be used for particular subjects or circumstances (*Dunning*, §8.13). The main value of item banking would be in assisting teachers with intermediate assessments, and it would be important in giving support to teachers' judgements in placing pupils in courses of study.

The *Dunning Report* also recommends that external tests should be shorter in duration than at present (*Dunning*, §7.5; §8.15). The reliability of an examination is, however, closely related to its length. If the external examination were to be used solely to provide the basis for scaling the internal assessments, it seems obvious that a shorter test would suffice, as the reliability of the average and of the measure of scatter are each greater than the reliability of the individual scores. But the Report recommends that in the early years of the new procedure the external examination should carry 75 per cent of the weight in determining the pupil's final mark (*Dunning*, §8.23). There is therefore a need for the external examination to be sufficiently reliable, and therefore long, to carry this weight. The Report envisages that in subsequent years the weight of the scaled internal assessment could be progressively increased from its initial 25 per cent (*Dunning*, §8.23); the length of the external examination could then be progressively decreased. The problem would then be one of effective coverage of the syllabus. This whole question of the length of the external examination is clearly one for research.

To sum up: linear scaling would appear to be the most valid and economical way of incorporating school assessments into the measures on which fourth year certificates are awarded. It has been found to work effectively even with small groups, but further research on this aspect is required. Item banking is a method on which much research is required.

Finally, we must always bear in mind that these methods and the modern computer which makes them possible are the tools in the hands of the assessors and not their masters, and that constant surveillance and improvement of their operations are necessary if progress is to be made.

References

Assessment for All: Report of the Committee to Review Assessment in the Third and Fourth Years of Secondary Education in Scotland. HMSO, 1977.

Elley, W. B. and Livingstone, I. D. *External Examinations and Internal Assessments.* New Zealand Council for Educational Research, 1972.

McIntosh, D. M., Walker, D. A. and Mackay, D. *The Scaling of Teachers' Marks and Estimates.* Oliver and Boyd, 1962.

Schools Council Examinations Bulletin 37. *Assessment by Teachers in Examinations at 16+.* 1977.

Scottish Certificate of Education Examinations Board. *Report on the Assessment of Practical Work in Science Subjects on the Ordinary Grade.* 1978.

THE ASSESSMENT OF ENGLISH—WHAT IS NEEDED?

Ernest Spencer was responsible for the recent SCEEB review of alternative means of assessing English and is now working on aspects of the use of language across the curriculum. In this paper he proposes a different model for assessment in English at O-grade, laying more responsibility upon the internal assessment by teachers responsible for the pupils' school work. He also suggests a weighting of internal against external elements considerably in excess of that suggested in the Dunning Report.

Although the burden of the paper is concerned with assessing a particular age range of pupils at a specific time in secondary education, the early part will be of interest to all who teach English at whatever stage. In discussing what we are attempting to assess, Mr Spencer opens up the whole question of the role of English in the curriculum. While he comes down on one side rather than the other for his particular purposes, perhaps we should ask ourselves whether the conclusion he comes to is equally valid in primary education or in the early years of secondary. Almost certainly there will be English specialists who will oppose his arguments and his conclusions even for the group with which he is most concerned.

A.W.J.

The Assessment of English—What is Needed?

E. Spencer

The views expressed in this paper are those of the author only: they do not necessarily represent the thinking of the Scottish Council for Research in Education or the SCE Examination Board.

What are we Assessing?

Assessment in some subjects appears to make fairly straightforward demands, which can be met by clear definition of the skills and knowledge regarded as comprising the subject, the composition of discrete test items dealing with each of the defined elements and the casting of these test items in multiple-choice form, so that marker unreliability is forestalled. This tidy model of assessment may have serious hidden faults: it may not, for instance, be apparent to anyone but the examiners that the selection of subject matter to be tested has depended, not only on professional judgements about what it was important to assess, but also, to a significant degree, on the effects of statistical evaluation after a pre-test, which might well have found certain items to be unusable, so leaving possibly very important aspects of the curriculum unassessed. Alternatively, items used without pre-testing might be invalid tests of the subject as specified. There may be a further and even more crucial concern: was the definition of the subject content adequate in the first place? To put this question another way, has an attempt to define a subject caused teachers and examiners to have too restricted a view of 'knowledge', so that they fail to test whether individual pupils can use it for their own purposes as well as remember it in the examination room?

English does not suffer from these dangers arising from 'disciplinarity'. Published English examination marks do look quite as definite as those of any other subject, but by comparison with some assessment systems, the process by which these marks are awarded is slapdash, for better or for worse, and part of the reason is the inability or unwillingness of English specialists to define precisely the nature of achievement in the subject. This 'failure' is partly due to realisation that the acquisition and use of language are highly involved processes, about which there is much that we do not yet know, and partly to a concern that these processes should not be over-simplified. Evaluation of any activity is, however, impossible unless the evaluator has criteria. With due regard for the complex nature of English work, anyone seeking to assess it must start with consideration of what he will regard as evidence of achievement. What, then, is the current state of thinking about language work in schools and what are the implications for assessment?

The place of language in schools can be considered with two kinds of approach, not necessarily in opposition to each other. Thought about language is concerned with the essential humanness of each individual, with his potentialities for reacting affectively to stimuli, for ordering and giving meaning to his experience, for relating to other people in various ways, for solving problems, for keeping several things in mind at once, for evaluating behaviour and ideas, for having purposes and for planning activity to achieve them. John Raven, in a recent book (Raven, 1977) has described such human qualities as 'competencies', and quotes extensive research findings to show that they are high on the list of educational priorities for most pupils and teachers. One is also concerned, in thinking about language, with a formalised (yet slowly changing) set of symbols and structures, which is a means of expressing, representing, influencing, ordering and, in some sense, controlling the individual's experiences so that his 'competent' action is facilitated. There is also that body of knowledge about language, culled from the various disciplines of linguistics and social science, 'its nature, the means by which it is acquired and developed, its role in socialisation, enculturation and schooling, its functional character as an instrument for thought', as Gatherer (1978) sums it up. Different emphases, corresponding to the 'competencies' approach and the 'language as a discipline' approach, can be found among English teachers and specialists, though, I repeat, their proponents are not necessarily opposed to one another. In describing the respective principal concerns of the two groups I am heavily indebted to discussion among the participants in the SCRE/SSRC Language and Learning Seminar held in January 1978 at the University of Stirling. (A review of the issues raised during this seminar is in Spencer, 1978.)

One emphasis, mainly represented at the Seminar by Tough, Tizard and Rosen, stresses the use of language in educational dialogue, regards language as the medium through which other things are learned, prefers to speak of 'communication' rather than language, being concerned primarily with the purpose and (in Tough's terms), 'function', or meaning, of language use. Some who adopt this approach would question whether language should be an educational area for children at all, suggesting that concentration on purposeful activity would lead to greater understanding by the child of his world and would be preferable to concentration on language. They would see a danger that too heavy an emphasis on language would reduce concern for learning in the broad sense of 'growing up', 'being human'. The school's role in facilitating 'humanness' is, in their view, to direct pupils to areas of experience they might otherwise miss and to ensure a more sustained dialogue and interaction with other people—teachers and pupils—who can help the individual to learn. Though the nature of 'educational dialogue' changes as children pass from nursery, through primary to secondary education—at the last stage it will sometimes be dialogue with oneself, in reflection on problems—the central point at all stages is that language is important as a means of communication, but what you are communicating about ('function') and with whom you are communicating (relationships) are the elements in the situation which facilitiate the learning of language structures. This emphasis might be summed up as a psycholinguistic one, concerned for the individual's learning in general, and for his engagement, with language-consciousness, in school experience and in purposeful activities: school work is to develop 'competencies' through experience and through language. There is a notable absence of references to subject disciplines in the arguments of those supporting this emphasis and, certainly, of reference to English itself as a discipline.

The Bullock Committee's advocacy of Language Across the Curriculum indicates its approval of this 'integrationist' general approach to language work. Gatherer (1978), in a paper presented to the Stirling Seminar, was the principal advocate of a different, more linguistic and more discipline-centred emphasis in thinking about language. Starting from the empirical fact that a subject called English is timetabled in schools, he argued that the teaching of that subject has suffered from too much freedom for teachers to make subjective judgements about what they should teach, and from the absence of a clearly defined curriculum content, which other subjects are assumed to possess. 'Curriculum development' in English to date has, he claims, been a series of shifts in pedagogical style, content remaining for the most part undefined. The Bullock Report has proved inadequate for the task of improving ways of developing a 'language for life' because its analysis of the English curriculum had in reality been an analysis only of pedagogy. Now it is both possible and timely for teachers to be given the resources they require for selecting and organising the *linguistic content* of English work, as well as the skills for teaching it, these resources consisting of 'Pedagogical Linguistics' (the 'curriculum matrix' of knowledge about language use) derived from the various disciplines such as linguistics, sociology and philosophy, insofar as they have been interpreted to relate to English.

The concern of 'English' is to develop language use only, to teach the pupils to listen, read, write and talk as best they can by encouraging these activities and reflection on them, the *content* of what is said or written being secondary. Content, experience, purposes and any linguistic skills (*e.g.*, in dialect) the pupil may already possess are important, but as motivators and as means by which the teacher can enter the pupil's linguistic world with a view to enlarging it, to take in previously unapprehended linguistic forms and structures. The peculiar aim of 'English' is linguistic efficiency in achieving *purposes*, rather than acculturation or the growth of general competencies, aims which, Gatherer points out, are claimed also by other subjects.

Most practising teachers of English would probably find the 'English as a discipline' approach attractive, though they might wish to place a little more emphasis on the general competencies as ends in themselves. Ten Brinke (1976), shows that almost all activity in 'mother-tongue' classrooms, including that designed to develop 'competencies' as defined by Raven, can be accounted for on the basis of two concepts, fiction (literature) and language, though he does include some of what have here been called 'general competencies' in a curriculum area 'complementary' to that which is specific to 'mother-tongue' and distinct from that of other subjects. The current thinking about curriculum of the Scottish Central Committee on English (SCCE) is stated in 'The Role of English in the Curriculum at S3 and S4' (the SCCE's submission to the Munn Committee) which quotes SCCE Bulletin No. 3, 'English for the Young School-Leavers' (SCCE, 1970) as defining the following aims of English teaching: 'first, to develop as far as the pupils are capable, the skills involved in reading, writing, speaking and listening; second, to provide experiences which will enrich the lives of the pupils and contribute to their personal growth'. Broad aims such as these still leave many value judgements and decisions about emphases, actual course-content and pedagogy to the teacher. Pedagogy will, of course, be strongly influenced by decisions about aims and course content, and criteria of assessment clearly derive from both.

What are the pedagogical implications of the 'competencies' and 'English as a discipline' emphases? The 'competencies' approach will be integrationist, seeking to develop linguistic skills incidentally as other things are learned, without special courses designed to 'give language'. The 'discipline' emphasis allows the *possibility* of 'language-giving' programmes. Definition of a curriculum content immediately entails the concept of deficit, which, in effect, refers to those elements in the total curriculum which a pupil does not have in his command, but which are needed to achieve his intentions (or his teacher's intentions). There is a strong implication in the 'discipline' approach that it is the English teacher's business to teach rhetoric, in the broadest sense—to consider what has made discourse effective to achieve various ends and to bring to the notice of pupils whichever techniques seem relevant to their particular purposes. Once the curriculum is circumscribed, the limits of the discipline defined, it is an easy step to think that the teacher should ensure his pupils' development by exposing them to courses which systematically cover all those possible rhetorical techniques of which they are ignorant but which form part of the field of study.

It should be noted that the possibility that English teaching might be regarded as 'giving language to pupils', though a very likely outcome of the 'discipline' emphasis, as is already obvious from the number of structured course-books on the market, is not an inevitable one. It would be possible to be concerned only with language use but to work always from the pupil's own purposes, his own language and his own reflections as they impose themselves on him.

The implication of the foregoing survey is that definition of clear and comprehensive criteria for the assessment of 'language performance' is a very difficult matter. It is, of course, possible to draw up criteria of achievement of some sort, but the more these relate to a 'non-disciplinary' way of thinking about English, the vaguer they are, and the more open to diverse interpretations. When they relate to a highly 'disciplined' view of English—e.g., when the criteria refer only to the ability to use certain grammatical structures—they may be less ambiguous, but also fail to take account of many important aspects of the use of language. Evaluation of the effects of any kind of course aiming to increase ability to use language is consequently problematical, whether it be of the 'intervention' type, designed to 'give' language to pupils in 'deficit', or not. Francis (1978) has reviewed a selection of 'intervention' and 'non-intervention' projects* for improving language performance in young children and has concluded that none had been able to evaluate their impact effectively because of lack of clarity about the nature of language development and its place in early education. We are not in a position to know that language deficit is really a matter of general experience or cognitive development: the research has shown only that 'language-intervention' programmes without cognitive aims have not had observable general consequences for intellectual development. The question seems to remain open, incidentally, whether deliberate attempts to extend vocabulary or improve command of structures might enable pupils to engage more fully in the educational experiences provided for them by schools. This might be a possibly more easily evaluated outcome, and an important one, since schools are so heavily committed to the use of language to influence and assess pupils' learning.

The central problem in evaluating the effects of school language work is that methods of measuring both cognitive development and language development are inadequate because we do not know enough about the nature of either, nor about the relationship between them, to devise other than simplistic tests which may well measure only the ability to pass those tests. The most pressing requirement for good assessment of language learning and teaching was firmly stated by Francis 'it is insight into the nature of these two activities as they take place in schools, and its prerequisites are much observation and description by teachers and researchers of how language is used in schools, with as much attention to structure as to function.'

Apart from its practical usefulness in motivating pupils and indicating their strengths and weaknesses, there is, therefore, a theoretical justification for concentrating on assessment as a description of achievement, and of achievement *in specific contexts*, about which as much as possible should be known and taken account of—the teachers' own use of language and his expectations of the pupil, the pupil's previous patterns of language use, the course being followed, the immediate purposes of the particular language use in question, the value judgements behind the teacher's curricular choices and his expectations. Some form of individual profile system of assessment is demanded by the state of our knowledge about language development,

---

*The projects reviewed were those reported in the following: Barnes, J. (Ed.) (1975), Gahagan, D. M. and Gahagan, G. A. (1970), Halsey, A. H. (Ed.) (1972), Rosen, C. and Rosen, H. (1973), Tough, J. (1976), Woodhead, M. (1976).

as well as by the need to 'diagnose' strengths and weaknesses in pupils' ability to use language in order to help them improve.

Assessment by description of achievement demands, on the part of the teacher, a high degree of consciousness of multivariate aspects of language functions as well as of the structures and vocabulary of the language, and it requires teachers to attempt the clear definition of criteria, a task in which Francis believed some professional researchers to have failed. There is the shortage of teachers' time, too, besides the daunting complexity of the task. The result of these difficulties in practice is that, alongside some superlatively creative and purposeful activity, a good deal of rather bitty, unplanned and directionless English work occurs. I am not arguing for inexorably predetermined English lessons. (A fuller statement of the kind of purposeful yet flexible course planning and assessment which I am advocating can be found in Spencer (1977)). There is, however, a need for English teachers in Scotland to accept and find time for the professional responsibility of assessing the value for individual pupils of the courses they are following, and to do it by coming to grips with the difficulties of describing success and development. Indeed, this responsibility should be regarded as a great opportunity to improve teaching. Despite many claims to the contrary, it is not the grading of pupils into 'A's', 'B's' and 'F's' in public examinations which maintains or improves standards—you can examine pupils till you and they are blue in the face, without having the slightest influence on standards. What does maintain and raise standards is teaching. And, while much effective teaching clearly occurs, there is no room for complacency. Many pupils in Scotland are following, even from S2, courses designed to push them 'en masse' through the O-grade examination in the hope that they will obtain Grade D or E, without any serious attempt ever being made during their secondary school career to evaluate exactly what they individually can do with language and to design programmes of work appropriate for their specific strengths and weaknesses. It is assumed that they will develop linguistically if they get texts to read and exercises to write. Good profile assessment would be invaluable in improving the standards of many of these individual pupils (and not only of those showing below average performance).

To summarise the kinds of radical change in assessment which I have been suggesting are needed, both for practical reasons and because of theoretical uncertainty about what is 'achievement' in language use, I offer the following quotation from my article 'Alternative to O-grade' (Spencer, 1977).

A genuinely educational change in attitudes to assessment in S4 would involve a shift from assessment for selection to assessment for other purposes and it might, perhaps, entail the view that assessments made in and by schools are of greatest significance before, not after, the pupil has left school. For instance, there is a strong argument that a statement of clearly defined achievement in various areas of work would be just as satisfying and 'motivating' as an A or B or C grade, and would give much more precise information about what needed special attention in the future. 'Profiles' of pupils' levels of attainment could be built up in, say, Personal Writing, Factual Writing, Persuasive Writing, Discussion Skills and Reading Skills of various types—response to whole texts, close reading of particular passages, 'survey' skills, etc. The experience of examiners distilled in instructions to markers is a helpful start in defining criteria of achievement, but it needs to be complemented by the teacher's knowledge of the pupil and of the particular purposes of the work in question. A spin-off advantage of having to define achievement in these fields would be the better planning and evaluation of their courses which the teachers would find themselves involved in. If English teachers are concerned with the personal development of pupils—and the theme of awareness of and confidence in one's own abilities and potentialities runs right through the SCCE Bulletins—some form of pupil self-assessment should also be important. This is a valuable way of getting pupils to make judgements about their own progress, which in combination with the views of their teachers, could be used as the basis for discussion about strengths and weaknesses, or, in a wider context, about careers guidance or personal development.

A Suggested Model for Discriminatory Assessment

Despite the problems of validity and reliability, discriminatory assessment goes on and must continue. There are pressing social requirements to grade pupils for selection by 'certification', and this process is associated in the minds of many people, albeit vaguely, with the desirable upkeep of academic standards. A second reason, more important however, is that we cannot avoid discriminating as we assess, however much we might wish to. We have no means of describing achievement except by comparison with what others have succeeded in doing. The criteria in 'criterion-referenced' tests are in fact knowledge or skills which somebody has achieved or exhibited before. 'Achievement' in English means the individual's development of language skill to the highest possible degree for him, but in order to know whether he has done this, we have to match him against the performance of others in the same activity. Comparison is the basic critical tool. The 'description of achievement' approach seeks to use comparison as a tool and not as an end in itself. In relating 'description of achievement' to discriminatory assessment, we are not seeking a classification of the pupils' ability or attainment in a general way, but rather trying to obtain a description of the different levels to which skills have been developed by different people. This description might then be used to help decide the next pedagogic step to take with a particular pupil, a description of whose own achievement is to hand. It may also, however, contribute to greater validity and reliability of whatever grading of pupils is necessary for selection.

What are the strengths and weaknesses of the methods normally used to effect discriminatory assessment?

The SCRE research (Spencer, 1979) dealt only with O-grade English, which has rather more problems than H-grade because of its very large and varied population. There are, however, many similarities between O-grade and H-grade examining techniques. The areas of work covered by both are Writing; Interpretation, including knowledge of language and summary; and Literature. Both examinations allow a fairly wide choice of composition topic and style, the H-grade offering options in discursive writing not available at O-grade. The H-grade also obliges all candidates to produce, in addition to the composition, a logically ordered piece of writing in appropriate style and register, based on information in note-form relating to a particular context and task—this part of the examination is usually known as 'the Report'. Both examinations set two passages for interpretation in 'traditional' form (*i.e.*, not employing multiple-choice questions). The H-grade paper requires pupils to show awareness of figurative and linguistic aspects of the text as well as of literal and inferential meaning, Literature (which is called 'Reading' at O-grade) is dealt with in both examinations by open, non-specific questions, in response to

D

which candidates may use any text which fits the question. At H-grade, candidates must answer in three of four sections, prose, drama, poetry and practical criticism of an 'unseen' poem (the only time a text is directly referred to by the questions). While the following comments on the strengths and weaknesses of the typical discriminatory assessment model refer directly to the O-grade English examination, I believe that they apply generally to any similar type of assessment and have relevance to the H-grade examination, and also to in-school assessments following a similar pattern.

The SCE O-grade examination has many advantages as a means of discriminating among pupils. Its administrative arrangements are well-tried and effective, and its nationwide currency ensures comparability of standards for all pupils. There is general satisfaction among both teachers and users of its results. It is very professionally set, and, over the years, attention has been paid to its 'washback' effect on the curriculum, so that, in principle, teachers are free to teach a wide variety of courses preparatory to the examination. The 'open' Composition and Reading questions are designed with this in mind. Also to the credit of the examination is the opportunity it affords some candidates to show their real worth—which they may have lacked the interest to reveal in school work—and its power as a motivator. The O-grade examination does, however, even as a discriminatory test, and apart from any actual undesirable influence on teaching, suffer from some faults. These are as follows:

a. The first fault is well-known: the examination is bound to be of limited validity, because it can sample only a small proportion of possible English work;

b. The second fault has also been notorious for a long time, but the public, including teachers, tend to accept it without much concern, as though thinking that modern methods of standardising marking put all things right—it is, of course, marker-unreliability. There is reason to believe that, despite the considerable efforts of the Board to standardise marking, some 25 per cent of candidates probably receive O-grade English marks which would differ by the full width of a band if a different marker marked their Paper I, Composition and Reading; in the case of a further 3 per cent or 4 per cent the discrepancy would be two full bands (Spencer, 1979). (Against this rather sensational information may be put the reminder that some 70 per cent of 70,000 candidates are quite reliably marked.)
    There may also be some significant unreliability in the Interpretation test. In the case of H-grade literature, there would almost certainly be very considerable disagreement among markers if several marked the same script;

c. The third fault is not well known, but it is of considerable importance: the O-grade examination is in reality a less fine discriminator than its published results make it appear. The markers produce a very bunched distribution of marks, with a standard deviation (SD) of, usually, about 12·5. This bunched distribution is then spread out by the SCEEB standardising procedure (commonly known within the Board as 'scaling') to provide a SD of 20. The real width of a *band*, in terms of marks actually awarded by markers is about $6\frac{1}{2}$ or, at most, 7 marks, and that of a range is 3 or $3\frac{1}{2}$; yet examiners, markers and teachers believe while marking that these widths are respectively 10 marks and 5 marks. Among the effects of this confusion are two particularly worth noting:

    (1) When the combined marks for Papers I and II total, say, 64, the award is

not B, range 7, as either marker would probably think, but A, range 5; or, when the raw marks total, say 35, the pupils gets, not D, range 11, but 'No award'.

(2) Discrimination at the level of *ranges* is in fact being made on the basis of 3 or 3½ mark categories, when it is normally held by experienced examiners that it is not possible in English to make educationally significant reliable distinctions between the quality of work produced by two pupils awarded within 5 marks of each other, because of the difficulties of defining in detail levels of achievement in English.

What of in-school discriminatory assessments? First, they are very powerfully influenced, both directly and indirectly, by the O-grade examination. Almost all schools copy the SCEEB model precisely in S4 examinations, and some also in S3, and it is well known that the format of the examination determines the tasks set for the pupils in their classwork. The indirect influence, subtle, but very effective, cannot, I suppose, be attributed solely to the O-grade, but rather to all external examinations, and it affects the teacher's way of thinking about assessment and about his work. Public examinations, especially if they are as syllabus-free as SCE O-grade, try to assess the attainment of general aims, or 'goals'—literacy, ability to understand a text, ability to write coherent continuous prose, ability to respond in a critical manner to literature . . .—as well as to produce a rank order of As, Bs and so on. Many school examinations and assessment procedures are set up with the same purposes in mind, so that they bear little or no direct relationship to the work pupils have been doing in class—that is frequently not assessed at all. The setter of the school examination believes that his job is to perform the same function as the O-grade examiners—to produce a ranking on which lines are drawn to differentiate those of high general attainment from those of average and low general attainment. As I have already suggested, clear definition of the difference between the attainment of someone near the top of the 'low' group and someone near the bottom of the average group does not exist. The view that examinations are about something much more general than the actual work pupils have done is not confined to S4—it can be found in S1 and S2, where the examination may have nothing to do with the projects carried out, and even 'continuous assessment' may really mean 'continuous tests' which perform the same sorting function as the O-grade. It is because teachers think of assessment as a general test for discriminatory purposes that examinations determine what is taught: they naturally want to place their pupils in as high a category as possible, so they teach what will come up in the exam, irrespective of its usefulness or appropriateness for the pupils as people at various different stages of development, with various different interests, and with various different kinds of achievement within their potential.

On a larger scale, the same kind of teaching goes on in S3 and S4: many pupils who might achieve more doing other things are pressed into 400 word compositions, O-grade interpretation tests and 20-minute response-to-reading answers as normal and invariable classwork. If these pupils obtain band E or 'no award' in the O-grade, can it be said that they have achieved anything—and if so, what? Discrimination has become more important than achievement, so that no realistic attempt is made to assess exactly what pupils can now do, describe it, and plan the next stage of work so that they can proceed, for instance, to exercise skills of which they have already shown awareness, but over which they need more sophisticated command.

Besides the tendency of discriminatory assessment to determine the curriculum, it also suffers in schools from the same problems of marker unreliability, 'bunching' of marks, and lack of precise criteria which affect the external examination.

Having arrived at the view that good teaching and learning needs 'description of achievement', but knowing that society requires assessment for certification, and, anyway, that the two types of assessment are interrelated, how can we get the best of both? How can we provide an assessment system which assures valid, reliable and comparable assessment across all schools at the certificate stage, encourages engagement in various kinds of English work and encourages the definition of clearer, more precise criteria of achievement for its various awards. In approaching this question I am thinking mainly of assessment in S1–S4, but I believe that in principle, the suggestions could apply equally to S5 and S6. There are three underlying principles:

1. If there is valid assessment of the content of a course designed to achieve general aims (or goals), there is also occurring valid assessment of those aims. 'Content' in English means language use to achieve various purposes in the work in hand. The requirement is that school assessment be directly related to a course of work planned to help the pupils achieve certain aims and also that it be related to modifications to the plan, due to the 'interactive process' between pupils and teacher—*i.e.*, that assessment should be of what was actually done, this being determined by the teacher's planning for whatever are his priorities *and* by the pupils' actual responses to the course, rather than by the content of a test which is known before the course is planned. The basic assessment model can be set out as follows:

    (1) *Flexible course-planning; (2) The course, which may depart from the plan as pupils' responses indicate that it would be necessary or useful to do so; (3) Assessment of achievement, either by 'description of achievement', or by comparative grading of pupils, A, B, C, on the basis of course-work or of an examination designed specifically to test the achievement of the purposes of the course.*

    Whether the assessment is for 'description of achievement' or for discrimination, it can be valid only if there is a clear statement of criteria against which to measure performance. Criteria are not immutable, and should be constantly adjusted according to knowledge about the nature of achievement in English and according to realistic awareness of what it is reasonable to expect of the pupils involved. It has already been argued that criteria are not easy to define in English. It is, nevertheless, the essential duty of the assessor to state what he regards as evidence of achievement, arriving at his definition by analysis of the purposes of the course (including, if possible, any unplanned work). O- and H-grade marking instructions and material produced by the SCRE research team and by the Scottish Central Committee on English might be helpful to teachers in this respect, but there is still a need for all involved, teachers and examiners alike, to seek to describe *positive* achievement at all levels of performance in more detail, in accordance with the argument of the first part of this paper;

2. The second principle is that 'objective' judgements really mean 'judgements taking account of as many informed views as possible'. Combinations of assessments are therefore likely to increase validity and reliability. The SCRE researchers found, (Spencer, 1979), that averaging Folio and O-grade marks led

to improvements in the correlation with the independent Criterion Test—and even in the cases of two schools whose Folio assessment was unsatisfactory, the average of Folio and O-grade scores correlated satisfactorily with the Criterion measure. The indications are that the effects of unreliable marking are much reduced by combining internal and external marks in equal weights. This leaves clear the possibility of a significant element of internal assessment for certification (which would also make 'description of achievement' more likely), even though the SCRE evidence showed that a few schools would not do the job well enough to be entrusted with assessment for certification on their own;

3. The third point concerns the need for an external element in assessment for certification, and the form it might take. The SCRE research evidence was that scaling against an external examination is necessary if any consistant severity or leniency by the school is to be corrected and if internal pass rates at each band are to match those of the O-grade. Neither excessive severity in one school nor discrepancies in pass rates in all schools were corrected by the Visiting Moderator scheme employed in the project. It has already been indicated that there is something unsatisfactory about the way in which some pupils are awarded O-grade bands, especially A's and 'F's'; it is, nevertheless, in the O-grade examiners that the right to set the standards resides, and, in any case, the simplest moderation process is scaling against an external examination.

What form should this external examination take? It needs to be as short as possible—and there is evidence that Writing and Interpretation, without Literature, would be adequate, though not quite as satisfactory as a test including literature questions. The SCRE research found that if the Interpretation is combined with a Writing task, the former might equally well be multiple-choice as 'traditional', as far as correlation with course-work assessment is concerned. There exist, however, in the minds of English teachers, grave misgivings about the appropriateness of multiple-choice tests in English; there are doubts about their validity, because it is sometimes hard to couch the questions one wants to ask in the 4-options form, and many fear that the use of such tests would have a bad effect on teaching, by reducing both open discussion and writing. If the latter could be avoided, multiple-choice tests might, nevertheless, be a valuable *addition* to assessment techniques in English; they should not supplant other kinds of close reading test.

Remembering that one of the aims of the exercise is to produce a system which will genuinely encourage curriculum planning and 'description of achievement', I suggest two 'sub-principles' here—(1) the external examination should genuinely *sample* areas of work, not try to allow the whole field to be covered; (2) since its primary purpose would be to form a common test for all, let it really be one— without choice of questions. The SCRE research (1979) seemed to suggest that marker-reliability would be greater if pupils were set a specified writing task without choice. There would be no unfairness in this if the internal assessment had at least equal weight with the external assessment and required pupils to write in several different styles for different purposes. If the external task varied from year to year within broadly defined limits, so that it would be impossible to tell exactly what would come up, the schools would have to undertake a variety of types of work, all of which would be internally assessed following the principles outlined in this paper.

The desired effect would thus be achieved of relating assessment more directly to work appropriate for particular groups of pupils selected by teachers from a range of possibilities defined by the broad aims of English teaching and by indications from SCEEB as to which tasks *might* appear in the external examination.

In summary, the assessment model I am proposing for S1–4 takes the following shape:

1. *Statement of general aims of English work;*

2. *Statement of various areas of work, types of activity, which would contribute to the achievement of these aims;*

3. *Statement of various areas of work, types of activity, which form a 'core curriculum' and which might, therefore, be required of pupils in the SCEEB examination (e.g., several types of writing and reading) or be essential elements in internal assessment for certification in S4 (some aspects of speaking and listening might be specified);*

4. *Selection by teachers of areas of work or activities from 2 and 3 above to suit their pupils and their own priorities, and flexible course planning based on these choices, leaving open the possibility of valuable unplanned activity arising as the course progresses;*

5. *In all of S1–4, assessment for 'description of achievement', for diagnosis of strengths and weaknesses, incidentally providing the means of evaluating the quality of the course;*

6. *At the end of S4, assessment for certification, by combined equally weighted internal and external assessment. The internal assessment might be of course-work or by examination designed to test achievement of the purposes of the particular course followed, and it should be made in the form of broad bands A to E (or F). The external examination might be without choice of question and the type of reading and writing tasks set could vary from year to year within the limits defined in accordance with paragraph 3 above.*
   The external test should be used to scale the internal assessment, to ensure comparability of standards in the internal assessment.

This model has not included any within-school assessment for discrimination prior to the end of S4. The ensuing paragraph is going to skate over this problem pretty rapidly. My thoughts on the matter are still primitive, but, for what they are worth, here they are—

The Dunning 'triple differentiation' approach (of Credit, General and Foundation levels) is obviously difficult, if not impossible, to apply to the English curriculum. In practice, however, differentiation after assessment of English constantly occurs throughout the secondary school. There is good reason to believe that, as a whole, this within-school discriminatory assessment is very variable in quality, as to both validity and reliability, so that there would be danger of pupils being committed to 'Foundation' or 'General' courses, for instance, which were not really suitable for them. If there is to be internal discriminatory assessment in S2, therefore, it should be possible for pupils to move easily to other courses during S3–4. Ideally, assessment for separation into the Dunning groups, or similar 'settings' for external examination, should be postponed until as late as possible in S4, but it might be difficult, even in English, to provide common courses suitable for all pupils up to that point. Many schools would wish to set pupils in S3 and 4. The best way of achieving this discrimination into three groups would be similar to the method proposed for certificate assessment. Course work, or an examination specifically designed to test it, could be graded, A–F, and combined, in equal weights, with similar grades for an examination common to all the pupils being graded—the latter is necessary to guarantee a common standard among classes.

The resulting rank order could be divided into 'Credit', 'General' and 'Foundation' groups on the basis of Dunning's proposed percentages of the population falling into these three groups, each school modifying the percentages of its pupils in each group according to the teachers' knowledge of the pupils from the 'description of achievement' assessment and to knowledge gained over the years about national standards from in-service courses, and feedback from SCEEB about the school's pass rates at each level. If assessment of this sort occurs at the end of S2, it is probably not necessary again until late in S4.

There are, of course, numerous difficulties in the assessment model I have put forward. I pass over the very major ones of lack of time to do all the work and the need for widespread in-service training, assuming, for the purposes of this paper, that adequate provision could be made. Some problems which would arise and regarding which teachers might wish to have guidelines are listed below:

The relative importance of assessment for different purposes and allocation of limited time available;

Criteria of achievement—what should be in a description of achievement? How detailed should national guidelines be?

Problems relating to course-planning, assessment planning and the teacher's freedom to design his own curriculum (this includes the problem of course elements which are not easily assessable how to avoid the danger of omitting these from the course because of the pressure of the plan, which will tend to concentrate on the measurable?) Are course-planning and assessment planning desirable? Or, would they, despite all efforts to the contrary, straitjacket pupils and teachers;

Similar problems relating to course-planning, assessment planning and the pupil's freedom to learn in the way best suited to him;

Question writing—how can they be made valid and unambiguous?

Problems with reliability of marking.

It would be possible to produce a booklet of guidance for teachers about these problems, but without the solid certainty that its advice was completely appropriate. There is still need for much thought and discussion among teachers, examiners and researchers about these matters. What advice and in how much detail is required? What other problems would occur if the model proposed were implemented? And what will be the alternatives if it is not? I hope I have shown that such discussion about assessment is, in fact, about concerns which are central to the teaching and learning process, to facilitate which the whole education system exists.

References

Barnes, J. (Ed.) (1975). *Educational Priority. Vol. 3: Curriculum Innovations in London's EPAs.* HMSO.

Francis, H. (1978). *Language Teaching Research and Its Effect on Teachers in Early Education.* As yet unpublished paper to the SCRE/SSRC Language and Learning Seminar, University of Stirling, January, 1978.

Gahagan, D. M. and Gahagan, G. A. (1970). *Talk Reform.* London: Routledge and Kegan Paul.

Gatherer, W. A. (1978). *Curriculum Development in the Field of English in Britain.* As yet unpublished paper to the SCRE/SSRC Language and Learning Seminar, University of Stirling, January, 1978.

Halsey, A. H. (Ed.) (1978). *Educational Priority. Vol. 1: EPA—Problems and Policies.* HMSO.

Morrison, C. M., Watt, J. S. and Lee, T. R. (Eds.) (1974). *Educational Priority. Vol. 5: EPA—A Scottish Study.* HMSO.

Raven, J. (1977). *Education, Values and Society.* H. L. Lewis (London).

Rosen, C. and Rosen, H. (1973). *The Language of Primary School Children.* Harmondsworth: Penguin.

Scottish Central Committee on English (1973). *Bulletin No. 3: English For the Young School-Leavers.* HMSO.

Scottish Education Department (1977). *Assessment for All.* (The Dunning Report). HMSO.

Spencer, E. (1977). *Alternative to O-grade in English and Assessment.* Strathclyde Region, Department of Education, Lanark Division.

Spencer, E. (1978). (Unpublished) Review of issues raised in the SCRE/SSRC Language and Learning Seminar, University of Stirling, January, 1978.

Spencer, E. (1979). *Folio Assessment or External Examination? The report of the SCEEB/SCRE project on Alternative Means of Assessing O-grade English.* The Scottish Certificate of Education Examination Board.

Ten Brinke, S. (1976). *The Complete Mother-Tongue Curriculum.* Longman.

Tough, J. (1976). *Listening to Children Talking.* London: Ward Lock.

Tough, J. (1977). *Talking and Learning.* London: Ward Lock.

Woodhead, M. (1976). *An Experiment in Nursery Education.* Windsor: NFER.

It is frequently said that mathematics is the easiest of all subjects in the curriculum to assess. It is claimed that in mathematics the answer is either right or wrong, that there is no room for opinion, that all deduction must be logical and cannot depend on subjective judgement, that the syllabus is more clearly defined than in any other subject and that there is less variation between schools than for any other subject in the curriculum. All of those things may be true yet this paper assessing mathematics makes it clear that mathematicians still have cause for concern and they would wish to bring about many more improvements before they are satisfied with both validity and reliability.

James Gillam is a Senior Examinations Officer and statistician with the Scottish Certificate of Education Examination Board and speaks with some authority on the problems facing the Board in assessing mathematics. However, his paper has much wider relevance and will be of interest to teachers at all stages in education who are concerned with subjects in which dealing with quantitative data and solving problems with numbers is a sizeable element.

A.W.J.

Assessment in Mathematics

J. Gillam

Assessment in Mathematics, as in other areas, cannot be considered without taking into account not only who and what is being assessed but—possibly of fundamental importance—why the assessment is being made. It may well be that an assessment is intended to fulfil more than one purpose and these purposes may have requirements which clash with each other. An obvious example is the requirements of a diagnostic and of a prognostic test. The former, being intended to identify areas where remedial attention is required, must be given at a time when it is possible to provide such attention; the latter is more effective the nearer it is to the choice of activity for which the prognosis is required.

The question of why the assessment is being made will recur frequently in this paper. Consideration of what is being assessed immediately focuses the attention on three possible areas: the cognitive, the affective and the psychomotor. Assessment in mathematics has traditionally been concerned with the first of these with occasional ventures into the last. Perhaps more attention should be given to the psychomotor domain. It is desirable to know whether a pupil can cope with the tools of mathematics tools which include not only the traditional instruments of rulers, compasses and protractor but the more recent additions of calculators.

Assessment in mathematics has long been concerned primarily with the more able mathematicians and has tended to neglect practical skills. Even for the more able however and certainly for the less able there is a need to emphasise practical skills and to relate the mathematics that is taught to the practical situation. For example much of the traditional work on fractions may be in need of rethinking. It is difficult to see much justification for the majority of pupils dealing with the problem of $2\frac{3}{4} \times 1\frac{7}{8}$. What may be more important is for example the realisation that a $\frac{1}{2}$ inch drill is intermediate in size between a $\frac{7}{16}$ and a $\frac{9}{16}$ drill; or that if a recipe calls for 6 oz of butter it is not necessary to have scales to find three-quarters of an eight ounce packet. This in its turn leads to the necessity of knowing that one quarter is one half of a half and that the best way of halving a rectangle is to mark the diagonals first. Such problems do not disappear with the adoption of metrication; when butter comes in 250 g packets and a recipe calls for 220 g it would be desirable that the pupil appreciates that 220 g is near enough $\frac{7}{8}$ of the packet. Conversion of miles to kilometres should lead to the appreciation that $\frac{5}{8}$ is $\frac{1}{2} + \frac{1}{4}$ of $\frac{1}{2}$; the giving of change should emphasise that addition and subtraction are equivalent. All of these remain within the classroom but it is arguable that mathematics should extend outside the classroom. The skills of measurement practised in small scale in the mathematics room can be practised on a larger scale in surveying and on a smaller scale in the field of precision measurement.

Advocacy of practical work is not new. The Scottish Education Department 'Note as to Mathematics' in 1936 stated that 'Special emphasis should be laid on practical work' and that 'Elementary exercises in surveying, including heights and distances, offer an interesting and stimulating form of the practical applications of mathematics'. It will be argued by many that such skills are not the province of the mathematics teacher but should be the concern of the teacher of science or geography or technical education and that the mathematics teacher is not equipped to venture into these fields. But over the years the mathematics teacher has had to move into many previously unknown fields and the area of practical measurement may be another such. If it is an area which is appropriate to mathematics teaching then it is an area appropriate to mathematics assessment. For what can be taught can be assessed. The assessment may be difficult; we may decide in the end that the cost in time or in money is too great. It should however be a conscious decision that we are voluntarily giving up an aspect of assessment, not simply a decision by default. If practical assessment were to be made, whether in the smaller field of geometrical drawing, curve sketching, or use of calculators, or in the other areas suggested above, then it is difficult to visualise such assessment being other than continuous and internal.

It should be emphasised here that advocacy of assessment does not necessarily imply advocacy of certification. The teacher who does not assess cannot know the effect of the learning experience that has been provided. It does not follow that he must label each individual pupil with an assessment; it does not even follow for this purpose that he need be concerned with the level of skill of the individual pupil. It is customary in assessment to realise the necessity for being satisfied with a sampling of content area; it is equally possible, though not often practised, to be satisfied with a sampling of pupils. In this sense we are essentially thinking of quality control of teaching and learning, and it is not unreasonable to suggest that the methods found adequate for quality control in industry may be applied in the classroom.

As has been stated above it is difficult to visualise assessment in the psychomotor domain being other than internal. Even as such however it is not without its problems. The assessment is completely comparable to the assessment of practical work in science subjects which has been reported on in a recently published report by the Board (Report on the Assessment of Practical Work in Science Subjects on the Ordinary Grade SCEEB 1978). Among the many difficulties are problems of lack of time, bias against individuals and lack of comparability of standards. These problems can to some extent be overcome but the assessment cannot be expected to have the reliability that teachers have come to expect of assessment in mathematics. In all assessment however there seems to be a kind of 'uncertainty' situation in that the more valid the assessment the less reliable it will be and the more reliable the less it will be valid.

Assessment in the affective domain is also largely untried. There are numerous statements of objectives in this domain ranging from the simplistic 'the pupil should enjoy mathematics' through that quoted in 'mixed-ability teaching in mathematics' (Schools Council Report. Evans/Methuen Educational 1977), viz.:

a. Developing appropriate attitudes to the subject including confidence, attention, willingness to learn and interest in the various aspects of mathematics—patterns, applications, problem solving;

b. Developing an appreciation of the significance of mathematics;

c. Developing an ability to experiment, to write up accounts of activity (as well as results) and general formation of appropriate work habits;

d. Developing an ability to formulate questions and extend problems to others that are more noted for their extensiveness than for their practicality.

Though there is no lack of statements of objectives in the affective domain, there is a lack of methods for their assessment. To some extent how much pupils 'enjoy' mathematics can be measured by noting how they 'vote with their feet' and in this connection it may be noted that mathematics—at least at the certificate level—is a male dominated subject. However examination presentation is not a measure only of choice; it is affected by school policy, by recognition of the 'career usefulness' of the subject. If assessment in the affective area is to be carried out it can probably only be done by a series of descriptive ratings provided by the class teacher that assess motivation, attitudes, work habits and other elements of affective behaviour. A basic problem of affective assessment is that the abilities being assessed are, even more than in the cognitive and psychomotor domains, a function of the interaction between the pupil and the teacher. It is the rule rather than the exception that a pupil may be interested and co-operative with one teacher and the reverse with another. A corollary is that any such assessment should be based on long term observation by a number of teachers. It might be unreasonable to consider the views of one teacher as objective but if the same rating is given by a number of teachers it would carry more weight. An unresolved problem is the standardisation of such observations between teachers and even more between schools. Such lack of objectivity may mean that assessment in the affective domain should be treated as a matter for internal school purposes only rather than form a part of any form of certification.

In the cognitive domain there is much more experience of methods of assessment than in either of the two areas previously considered. Here again however the selection of a method of assessment should depend on the purpose of that assessment and there are a number of such purposes. Criticism of assessment often arises from a misconception of the purpose or because the assessment is being used for more than one purpose. There are at least six purposes that can be identified for assessment, viz.:

a. the measurement of achievement;

b. selection;

c. prognosis;

d. diagnosis;

e. motivation;

f. improvement of teaching.

The requirements of each of these may differ and it is hardly surprising that one instrument is unsatisfactory to carry out all six purposes at one time. Thus, for example, if a test is intended for prognosis, in particular say for selection at the beginning of S3 those pupils who are likely to be successful in Higher Mathematics in S5, then regard must be had to the fact that nationally only about 10 per cent of the age group fall into this category. A satisfactory test for this purpose must therefore be able to discriminate well between the top 10–15 per cent and the remainder. The greatest discrimination in a test is achieved when half the candidates at the ability level where the discrimination is to be made are successful and half unsuccessful. It is obvious that a test designed to satisfy that criterion is unlikely to motivate pupils at a lower level of ability.

There are a number of different aspects of assessment of cognitive objectives that can be considered in addition to the purpose of the assessment. The assessment may be terminal or periodic or cumulative; it may be internal or external and may be based on an internal or an external syllabus; it may consist of short answer questions, including possible fixed response items, or may demand more sustained working; it may be oral or aural or written; it may be specific to one part of the ability range; it may attempt to cover the whole of an age group. The remainder of this paper will attempt to look at each of these aspects and consider some of the advantages and disadvantages attached to them. It is important to appreciate that there is no correct answer to the problems posed by assessment. Each method that has been adopted because there are reasons in its favour and the multitude of existing practices testifies to the fact that no one method is a panacea.

The arguments in favour of short questions as contrasted with those demanding more sustained working are that their use allows more questions to be used in a given period of examination and can therefore ensure a wider coverage of the syllabus area. Any assessment is by necessity a sampling of the specific objectives of the course and the wider that sampling the more valid can be the assessment. Thus using short questions, one hour's examining could range over some 40 topics whereas longer questions would restrict the coverage to five or six areas. Moreover short questions can explore in depth the extent of a candidate's abilities whereas with a long question the candidate who cannot complete the first step cannot show his abilities in succeeding steps. A blank answer sheet can provide very little information. The demands made on a pupil by a mathematical question are sometimes not sufficiently appreciated. As an example consider a sustained question which might well be used at S4 level with pupils from the higher ability level.

'Three ships A, B and C are positioned so that A is 18 km from B on a bearing of 035°, the bearing of C from B is 136° and the bearing of A from C is 330°. How far is B from C?'

The pupil first has to draw a sketch of the situation. This involves knowing the meaning of the term 'bearing' and being able to construct, at least approximately angles of a given size. He then has to realise that it is appropriate to calculate the sizes of other angles not given, making use of the properties of parallel lines. Next he must realise that he has sufficient information to 'solve' a triangle and that the appropriate tool to use is the Sine Rule. He must recall that rule, manipulate it into a useable form and finally make use of mathematical tables or a calculator to carry out the necessary working. There is no way in which the pupil who fails at the first hurdle by being ignorant of the meaning of bearing can show the ability that he may possess to clear the remaining hurdles with ease. That some pupils can clear all these hurdles reflects credit on their ability and on the ability of their teachers to teach them but it is not surprising that few pupils do in fact succeed. It is not difficult to replace the one question by six, each one testing one aspect of the problem. However it cannot be denied that something is lost by such a replacement and there are those who would argue that what is lost is the essence of mathematics. They would argue that mathematical ability is measured not by competence at individual tasks but by success at appreciating the whole of a situation and selecting the appropriate ways of dealing with it. Obviously if one is interested in the diagnostic element of the assessment this argument will carry little weight; if in the prognostic element it merits further consideration the single question may well motivate the more able, it will certainly discourage the less able. As has been already stressed the 'why' of the assessment will go a long way to determining the 'how'.

Within the area of the short answer type of question there is disagreement about whether completion or fixed-response format is the more desirable. It may be argued that mathematics is of all subjects the easiest in which to write fixed response items and the one in which they are of least use. Opponents of fixed-response items would claim that to test whether a pupil can expand $(x + 2y)^2$ as $x^2 + 4xy + 4y^2$ it is better to ask him to expand it than to select the correct expansion from 5 alternatives. That there is some measure of truth in this is shown by the results of testing two similar items on similar groups of S1 pupils.

One was

x.x.y.2 can also be written as
A 8xy B $2x^2y$ C $2x^2y^2$ D $2xy^2$ E 4xy;

the other

a.a.b.4 can also be written as
A 2a4b B 8ab C $4a^2b$ D a^2b^2 E $2ab^2$

In the former 63 per cent of candidates chose the correct answer, in the latter 22 per cent. The inclusion of distractor A in the second, which attracted 40 per cent of the pupils turned the question from an easy one to a difficult one. The response to a multiple choice item depends not only on the stem of the item but also on the distractors. Whether or not this matters depends on the purpose of the test. If all we are concerned with is rank-ordering the pupils then it may not be important. There is considerable evidence that the rank order achieved by a fixed response test is as close to that achieved by an extended response test as it would be reasonable to expect. If however the test item is being used to discover which pupils know that x.x.y.2 = $2x^2y$ or a.a.b.4 = $4a^2b$, then there are obviously deficiencies. The fixed response item then, has drawbacks, but so too has the completion item. An Ordinary grade Arithmetic question recently asked candidates to 'Express as a single fraction $4\frac{1}{2} \times 1\frac{2}{9}$'. Among the answers recorded were $\frac{11}{2}$, $5\frac{1}{2}$, $5 \cdot 5$, $\frac{99}{18}$, $5\frac{9}{18}$, $5\frac{162}{324}$, $5\frac{81}{162}$, $\frac{1782}{324}$, $\frac{891}{162}$, $4\frac{27}{18}$, $\frac{5 \cdot 5}{1}$ and $\frac{49 \cdot 5}{9}$. There were also a large number of wrong answers. It could be argued that the only acceptable answer is $\frac{11}{2}$ but it is probable that few mathematics teachers would not accept $5\frac{1}{2}$. Exactly where in the set of 12 answers given above the line should be drawn would probably vary from marker to marker, and an obvious degree of marker unreliability would exist. Such unreliability is much more easily eliminated in a school situation where there can be on-going discussion than in a national examination. It can also be argued that by a careful statement of the question such difficulties can be eliminated. However it is always easier to be wise after the event than before. Even the previously quoted example 'Expand $(x + 2y)^2$' could produce as answers $(x + 2y)(x + 2y)$; $x(x + 2y) + 2y(x + 2y)$; $x^2 + 2xy + 2xy + 4y^2$; x.x + x.2y + 2y.x + 2y. 2y. Are any of these acceptable?

A further advantage in the national scale of fixed-response tests over short answer tests comes in ease of marking. The former can be computer marked, the latter have to be marked either by clerical staff if there is no doubt about acceptable answers or by teachers if subject expertise is necessary. Marking of a one hour objective test by computer for 30,000 candidates would cost about £500; the same job done clerically would cost £1,500; sent out to marking-by-subject experts the cost would be of the order of £7,000. No one would argue that cost should be an over-riding argument but neither can it be ignored. A further benefit of computer marking is that it allows immediate analysis of responses. This in its turn allows comparisons between years and between parts of a syllabus. It is true that the same can be achieved for free-response questions but the costs then become prohibitive. The scale on which testing has to be conducted will then be an additional factor to be considered along with the purpose of the test when deciding on the format to be adopted.

It is sometimes put forward as an argument against fixed-response testing that this form of assessment encourages pupils to guess. To some extent 'guessing' is to be encouraged rather than discouraged in mathematics. The pupil who 'guesses' that a solution of $x^{100} + 5x = 1$ is about 0.2 is displaying mathematical ability of a high order. He is still displaying mathematical ability when he chooses 0.2 from five given options. The concern is not about this kind of guessing but about 'blind' guessing where a candidate simply marks a response at random. It is not unreasonable to suggest that blind guessing occurs only when pupils lack motivation or are presented with situations that are far beyond their capabilities—the latter may of course be one cause of the former. That assessment instruments should be suitable for the pupil being tested is pertinent when considering whether one 'test' can be appropriate for the whole of an age group. This question may however not be the correct one to ask. A preliminary question is whether one syllabus is appropriate for the whole of an age group. If the answer is that it is not—and most if not all mathematics teachers would agree that it is not—then one assessment instrument will not be appropriate. There is an obvious difference here between mathematics and some other subjects. It is possible in history to ask for the causes of the Second World War and to expect different kinds of answer from different pupils. Traditionally, mathematics questioning has not been of this type. When we ask a pupil to solve $x^2 + 5x + 3 = 0$, there is one form of response that is expected from all pupils who have been taught the technique. It is possible to devise questions of a different kind; for example we might ask them to comment on the number facts $\frac{2}{3} - \frac{1}{2} = \frac{1}{2.3}$; $\frac{3}{4} - \frac{2}{3} = \frac{1}{3.4}$; $\frac{4}{5} - \frac{3}{4} = \frac{1}{4.5}$; $\frac{5}{6} - \frac{4}{5} = \frac{1}{5.6}$ or from the same given facts we could ask

1. What is the value of $\frac{6}{7} - \frac{5}{6}$?

2. What is the value of $\frac{99}{100} - \frac{98}{99}$?

3. Generalise these results

4. Prove the truth of the generalisation

That these questions are not asked probably stems from the dilemma of trying to reconcile the claims of mathematics as a subject in its own right and as a service subject. The latter aspect is of such importance that it leaves little time for the former. If the service aspect of mathematics is accepted as being of prime importance then it follows that mathematics assessment will continue to be syllabus dominated, and the assessment appropriate to groups of pupils will diverge. Obviously it is possible to devise assessments that would allow all pupils to do some questions and some pupils to do all questions, but only at the expense of boring the more able and discouraging the less able. The domination of assessment by syllabus in mathematics is well illustrated by consideration of assessment at Higher and Sixth Year Studies level. If a pupil who had completely mastered the Higher Mathematics syllabus and had gone no further were faced with one of the Sixth Year Studies Mathematics papers—say Paper II—then he would be able to score few if any marks on it. In no other subject is this true to the same extent. It is not really meaningful to consider 'syllabus-free' assessments in mathematics, not because such are not possible, but because external pressures rule them out.

If a common assessment instrument is ruled out, is it possible still to envisage a common assessment measure? Those who argue that it is are implying that all possible questions in mathematics can be ordered so that for a pupil of given 'mathematical ability' there is a decreasing probability of a correct response according to the displacement of the question along such an ordering. To a limited extent such a concept is not unacceptable; the multiplication of two single digit numbers would occur in such an ordering before the multiplication of two two digit numbers, and a pupil scoring 60 per cent on the latter would expect a higher score on the former. Even this however may not be so. If the 40 per cent failure rate in two digit multiplication arose from ignorance of the multiplication facts for 7, say, then it would be matched in the single digit multiplication test. Moreover mastery of single digit multiplication gives no guarantee of any success in two digit multiplication, nor does failure in the latter imply success in the former. The problem is difficult when restricted to one topic; it is even more difficult when trying to place topics in such an ordering. It is not so long ago that vectors were considered appropriate only in a university mathematics course; now they may well be taught in primary school. Of course the kind of question on vectors for these populations differs but it seems difficult to place topics as such in any such overall mathematical ordering. Assessment in mathematics is concerned with two aspects: an underlying mathematical ability and the application of that ability to particular syllabus areas. Examining tends to measure the former only as a by-product of the latter. So long as that state exists it is difficult to see the possibility of comparable awards in widely differing syllabuses. Whether it should continue to exist depends on the purpose of mathematics teaching. For many pupils the content is of fundamental importance; it is important to know whether pupils can cope with solution of simple equations or solution of quadratic equations or solution of trigonometric equations. For others, who are not going to use mathematics, it may be that what is important is mathematical thinking divorced as far as possible from syllabus content.

As has been seen, the question of assessment in mathematics cannot be divorced from consideration of syllabus. It may therefore be appropriate to consider to what extent the syllabus should be externally defined. The arguments in favour of an internal syllabus element are that it allows reflection of local conditions, and that it allows the teacher to concentrate on these areas that interest him and/or the pupils. Against it can be argued that mathematics is universal, not local, and that while no-one would dispute the teacher's right or duty to pursue interesting topics, these topics as such should not form part of an external assessment, since by their nature they negate the possibility of comparability. Such digressions from the external syllabus could be of benefit in two ways: an increased motivation and in the possibility of seeing applications of the external syllabus in new situations. On the other hand while mathematics is universal it may well be that it is unfair particularly at the lower end of the ability range to assess mathematical objectives other than in the context in which they are taught. Certainly if the choice is between testing the objective without any context and testing it in different contexts for different groups, then the latter is preferable. The increase in validity will be sufficient to outweigh the loss of reliability. While there is room for argument about the desirability of internal syllabus, there is less room for argument about the desirability of internal assessment. The principle of internal assessment has long been accepted in the provision of an appeals procedure in certificate examinations. It is generally accepted that the reliability of the composite of two measures will usually be greater than the reliability of either. There is room for debate as to the 'weighting' of the internal and external elements, and whether the incorporation of an internal element can allow the shortening—with the consequent decrease in reliability—of the external element. It is also for debate whether the expense both in terms of time and money involved is worthwhile. In part such a decision will depend on the degree of discrimination that is wanted. If it is desirable, as is apparently the case in Scottish Certificate of Education examinations, to classify candidates into 14 ranges, then more information is required about all candidates than is necessary if a two range classification—pass and fail—is required. On the other hand a simple pass-fail system encourages the idea that assessment can be precise, that it is possible to separate the successful from the unsuccessful. Mathematics is less affected by problems of marker reliability than other subjects and it can be argued that in mathematics it is possible to say that a candidate rightfully gained the marks necessary to pass; but for many whether or not he would gain the same status on a slightly different sampling of the syllabus must be doubtful. There are probably candidates who know that sin 2x = 2 sinx cosx, but don't know that cos 2x = cos²x — sin²x. There are others who know the latter but not the former. Which one appears in an examination may for some of these candidates separate the passes from the fails. Because a pass-fail system is suspect there is a demand for grading, and grading demands discrimination. The search for discrimination leads to assessment systems where much of the content is effective only for the top of the ability range being assessed—where in fact discrimination may be totally unnecessary. This in turn leads to tests incorporating the idea that the 'pass-mark' should be 50 per cent—that 'half right is all right'. It is arguable that all that should be asked of any assessment system is to identify three categories. Those who have achieved the objectives, those who have not and a group in between about whom we are doubtful. In terms of internal testing this would mean identifying three groups: those who are ready for the next stage of mathematics; those who require remedial work before, if ever, attempting the next stage; and those who can be allowed to proceed to the next stage, but require in addition reinforcement of the current stage.

Going on to the next stage implies that assessment should be periodic. It does not necessarily follow that certification should make use of such periodic assessment. There are many purposes of assessment of which certification is only one. The arguments against periodic assessment are solely in respect of the part it should play in certification, and in the role of certification as a selecting process. It is argued that when a university or a further education college or an employer demands a qualification in mathematics, the interest is not in what the candidate could once do but has forgotten, but in what has been retained. For this purpose the assessment should be made as late as possible. However assessment in mathematics is used not only as a guarantee of subject content—and as such it can never be an absolute guarantee—but also as a guarantee of general ability in mathematics. For this purpose it may be sufficient that the assessment should guarantee not that the pupil can, say, use trigonometry to solve a right angled triangle, but that he was capable of being taught to do so—and in this periodic assessment has a role to play. Problems arise when an attempt is made to combine periodic assessments of the same skill. If different pupils have periodic assessments in one case of 5, 5, 5, 5, in a second of 3, 4, 5, 8, in a third of 8, 5, 4, 3, and in a fourth of 7, 3, 3, 7, are they all equal? If not, which is the 'best'? Periodic assessment can provide an incentive in the early stages of a course, but, if it is cumulative, what incentive can there be for a pupil who knows at the end of S3 that no matter how well he does in S4 his overall result can never reach a 'satisfactory' level?

There are many other aspects of assessment in mathematics that have not been touched on. How can the least able be assessed? Is certification of such pupils necessary or desirable? Assessment is certainly not only possible but desirable. What can be taught can be assessed. The problem is not in assessment as such but in producing an assessment that will be comparable between schools. Is there an optimum length for an assessment? It is probable that for the less able it is unrealistic to think in terms of a single two hour examination session. Perhaps a series of short assessments—some written, some oral and aural, some practical—is a better pattern.

This paper has not produced, and was not intended to produce, any answers, but rather to pose a series of questions, and in particular to emphasise that the most important question on assessment is 'Why is the assessment being made?'

ASSESSMENT IN SCIENCE

Science is taught essentially through practical methods; pupils are required to use experimental techniques to test hypotheses that they have formulated about the behaviour of the materials they are examining and, from the data they obtain, either to reject the hypothesis, modify interest in it, or accept it as valid and build it into theories and generalisations. Carefully controlled 'guided' discovery can allow pupils to establish most of the basic concepts of the sciences by behaving as scientists. In the course of the work they learn many of the processes of scientific thought and action which form the backbone of any good science syllabus. Qualitative relationships, processes, knowledge, the formulation and use of concepts, theories and generalisations, attitudes and practical skills are all learned and should somehow be assessed. There are within science the elements of assessing mathematics, English the social subjects and even the creative arts, all involved in some way. At the same time some of what is required to assess science is also needed to assess Home Economics and Technical Subjects. The problem of practical work is of particular interest since so little effort has been made to assess it realistically.

Considerable changes have been made in recent years in the methods used to assess the sciences in SCEEB examinations and other subjects have or are being evaluated. Dr Dennis Gunning, for example, recently looked at possible ways of assessing practical work as part of the external examination.

Dr Kellington is well placed to discuss the problems of assessing the sciences. He is Senior Lecturer in Physics at Notre Dame College of Education, has recently evaluated the new form of the Integrated Science Syllabus, producing his own criterion-referenced tests to do so, and he is at present Chairman of the Physics Panel of the Examination Board.

In his paper he discusses at some length the various problems met with in attempting to assess all that science tries to teach, including the difficulties of continuously assessing practical work. He describes an alternative method of assessment for all science courses, including the general certification conducted by the SCEEB, incorporating the techniques of criterion-referenced testing used in his own evaluation project. In such a system, he maintains, science can be more effectively and fairly tested and difficulties diagnosed. Item banking, criterion-referenced testing and standardisation—all subjects of other papers—are elements in the programme outlined. He argues that, using techniques such as he proposes allied to teaching based on ideas of mastery learning, pupils would be much more motivated. (He is not alone in making such claims).

He does not discuss at any length the resources needed to devise and sustain such courses nor the non-teaching time needed to prepare lessons and monitor progress, yet they must be considerable. Can we, ought we to, afford them? Is this one means of coping with the surplus of teachers created by the drop in pupil numbers already visible in primary and soon to be affecting secondary schools also? How far can the suggestions for such a system in science be applied to other areas of the curriculum?

A.W.J.

Assessment in Science

S. H. Kellington

Introduction

In common with all academic subject areas, it would be highly desirable for examinations in science to assess those aspects of its study which are considered to be the most important to the candidates. Unfortunately, also in common with other subject areas, it is necessary to limit the scope and nature of examinations in science to include only those aspects which can be assessed with both reliability and validity. Additional constraints apply to national examinations when cost and feasibility figure prominently.

Absence of suitable techniques of examining, however, are not responsible entirely for limitations in science examinations. It is usual, for example, for examinations to be based on a definitive syllabus. All too often, syllabuses lack the necessary precision for this purpose. It is also usual for examiners to attempt to reflect in their papers the underlying aims and philosophy of a course. Unfortunately, these are rarely stated with sufficient clarity to form an adequate basis for the design of an examination.

Before assessment in science is considered, therefore, it is pertinent to review, briefly, the kind of scientific study which is deemed to be appropriate at the secondary level of education. Following this review, aspects of scientific study which have been included in science examinations are considered, and aspects which have been neglected are highlighted. Finally, possible methods, by which aspects at present neglected may be assessed, are described, and an alternative approach to assessment is introduced. This approach is included in view of recent recommendations that a greater proportion of pupils should follow courses leading to certification, and that schools should be more actively involved in the assessment process (*Dunning Report; Assessment for All:* 64).

Although this paper is concerned, primarily, with secondary courses of science in Scotland, and corresponding assessment procedures, implications for tertiary courses in science are mentioned briefly. Links to primary education, although rather more tenuous, can be made through the consideration of skills which can be developed in the primary school, for subsequent use in secondary science courses.

Scientific Study in the Secondary School

During the 1960's, there was intense activity in the development of new science courses for the secondary school. This activity began in the United States and was initiated by the reaction to the launching, by the USSR, of the first 'Sputnik'. It was argued that a new approach to the teaching of science could encourage pupils of high ability to study science and, ultimately, to contribute to the development of advanced technology. In the United Kingdom, developments took place in parallel with those in the United States. Among the most significant new courses were the Nuffield science programmes in England and the 'alternative' syllabuses for chemistry and physics in Scotland. A corresponding new syllabus for biology followed a few years later. Such has been the rapid development of courses in the last twenty years that the recent report of the International Clearinghouse (Lockard, 1977), which outlines new projects in science and mathematics education, developed during this period, runs to more than 500 pages.

The 'traditional' courses in science which were devised before the 1960's were concerned, primarily, with enabling pupils to acquire knowledge of scientific facts and theories, knowledge of laws and their application to problems, and an understanding of simple technology which was related closely with the subject matter of the courses (Klopfer, 1971). In general, the subject matter was presented in discrete units, and little effort was made to relate the content in one unit with that in others. Teaching approaches were limited, in many cases, to the presentation of facts, theories and laws, which were intended to be accepted by pupils as correct or to be 'proved' by appropriate laboratory exercises. In spite of the extensive use of laboratory work, in many courses, and the including of theories and laws in the course material, emphasis was placed only rarely on use of the 'scientific method' of investigation.

The 'new' science courses developed during the 1960's and 1970's stand in sharp contrast to the traditional courses, described above. The most obvious difference, perhaps, is in the organisation of the subject matter. In physics courses, for example, a large proportion of the traditional areas of 'heat', 'light' and 'sound', which were described usually in separate parts of a syllabus, tend to be included within a unifying theme of 'waves'. This theme may include a study of several wave phenomena and lead to an examination of the similarity of and differences between various kinds of waves. In traditional courses of biology, as a further example, the topics of blood circulation, nervous system, digestion, and food and water movement in plants were often treated separately. In new courses, such topics are often included within a unifying theme of 'transport systems'.

The main purpose, in the grouping of traditionally discrete topics into unifying themes, is to illustrate the nature of scientific enquiry (Rogers, 1970; Nedelsky, 1965). In particular, the processes of formulating hypotheses and developing theoretical models are emphasised and applied to several phenomena within a given theme. Advantage is also taken of this grouping to provide several examples for the testing of hypotheses and models by experiment. Techniques of 'discovery learning' (Ausubel, 1968) and 'guided discovery' are advocated frequently as being appropriate for the development of the skills required for scientific enquiry.

This emphasis on methods of scientific enquiry can be costly in time, however, and some of the scientific facts contained in traditional courses are omitted. The sacrifice is made to allow more time for pupils to acquire the abilities which are necessary for the solving of problems and the carrying out of investigations in a scientific manner.

Although the amount of material in new science courses tends to be less than in traditional courses, high demands are made on pupils in terms of intellectual and practical skills. Not least of the skills required are those relating to the manipulation of modern laboratory equipment. In addition to intellectual and practical skills, however, attempts are made to encourage pupils to acquire appropriate attitudes to scientific investigation, and the role of science in society. In particular, objectivity in observation and towards experimental evidence are considered to be important, and it is hoped that an appreciation of science as a human endeavour, with profound consequences for society, will be acquired.

In comparison with traditional courses, little emphasis is placed on technology as a way of producing motivation. It is hoped that the challenge to pupils of approaching problems scientifically and acting, even if only to a limited extent, as a scientist will provide sufficient motivation.

Concurrent with the rapid development of new science courses, and possibly as a consequence of it, there has been a rapid growth in the development of methods for specifying the intended outcomes of courses. Although such development has not occurred solely for science courses, its results have been valuable for science courses in particular. One of the benefits of this work has been the categorisation of educational objectives (Klopfer, 1971) and their use in communicating the intentions of curriculum developers to teachers and pupils. The value of objectives as a basis for assessment procedures is considered in a subsequent section.

Development of Assessment in Science

It is clear, even from the very brief comparison of traditional and new science courses given in the previous section, that the content, aims and philosophy of science courses have changed substantially during the last two decades. It might be anticipated, therefore, that corresponding changes in assessment procedures would have been effected to take account of expected changes in pupils' achievement. Although some modifications have been made, and some new techniques have been introduced, several important aspects of the new science courses are not represented in current examination procedures. In general, the development of examination procedures has been slow on account of two main factors; the need to be satisfied that new procedures are reliable and valid, and the difficulty of assessing achievement in certain important aspects of courses. Moreover, delays in matching assessment procedures to the new courses may well have affected the implementation of the courses themselves, since the nature of an external examination can exert a substantial influence on the way in which a course is presented by teachers. The relationship between courses and assessment is explored further in the final section.

The most significant development in certificate examinations for science subjects in Scotland has probably been the introduction of objective testing (Houston, 1970). This has been in operation in chemistry and physics since 1971, and will be introduced in biology in 1979. Although leading to financial economies in the marking of examinations, the introduction of objective testing was justified on educational grounds. One advantage of this form of testing is that each question can be linked to a specific educational objective for a course, if such objectives exist, and can be designed to assess the ability of candidates to display a particular intellectual skill, as well as knowledge of a particular area of content. Another advantage is that a relatively large number of questions, often 40 or 50, can be attempted by candidates in approximately one hour, and this can lead to high reliability.

Although many skills, including recall, comprehension of knowledge, application and analysis, can be assessed by objective tests, some skills which are emphasised in new courses cannot be assessed adequately by this technique. In particular, any skill requiring candidates to communicate explanations or interpretations cannot be assessed although candidates can be asked to select from given alternatives. It is mainly for this reason that certificate examinations also include other kinds of tests.

Other parts of certificate examinations in science have evolved rather slowly since the alternative courses were first implemented. Over the years, much use has been made of questions requiring short written answers and the solution of numerical problems. Typically, the questions are highly structured, with each part requiring answers which are clearly delineated for the candidates. The length of required answers increases, in general, in the progression from examinations on the Ordinary Grade, through Higher Grade to the Certificate of Sixth Year Studies. Recently, however, in science examinations on the Ordinary and Higher Grades, considerable care has been taken during the construction of objective and extended answer papers to include questions requiring the display of certain specified skills. By carefully selecting questions in terms of these skills, as well as of subject areas, it has been possible to construct papers with approximately the same demands from year to year. One of the benefits of this procedure has been the availability to teachers of statements regarding the skills which the examinations are designed to assess.

The most recent development in this kind of test has taken place in chemistry on the Ordinary Grade. Candidates are required to attempt all the questions in the paper and each question is designed specifically to assess abilities in the areas of knowledge, comprehension, application and enquiry. Of particular significance is the attempt being made to assess candidates' ability to seek new knowledge through scientific enquiry. Questions are being included, moreover, to assess the ability to formulate hypotheses, to devise experimental procedures to test hypotheses, and to evaluate hypotheses in the light of experimental results.

One point to bear in mind, when considering the attempts being made to match examinations to the aims and philosophy of a new science course, is that the examiners are faced with a dilemma. In order to assess a candidate's ability to formulate a hypothesis, for example, it is desirable to present an unfamiliar test situation so that the candidate is unable to recall an appropriate hypothesis from previous knowledge. It is almost impossible to present an unfamiliar situation, however, since examinations, at the present time, are based on definitive syllabuses, which state the subject matter to be examined. Such syllabuses, which are more appropriate for traditional science courses, consequently restrict the choice of test situations to content which should be familiar to pupils and teachers. At the present time, attempts are being made to solve this dilemma by introducing some new aspect into test situations while ensuring that both the subject matter and techniques required should be familiar. New types of syllabus are under investigation, however, and it is possible that a more satisfactory solution to the dilemma may be found in the near future.

Assessment of pupils, during certificate courses, has tended to rely on questions of the type included in certificate examinations. It is common for pupils to be tested once in each term on questions which have been set in previous certificate examinations. Some assistance has been given to schools, however, by the examination board which has provided sets of objective tests.

A form of assessment approaching 'continuous assessment', (*Dunning:* 24) has been developed for the Integrated Science (Curriculum Paper 7, HMSO) course, which is followed by many pupils in Scotland during their first two years in the secondary school. At the end of each of the fifteen sections of the syllabus, it is common for pupils to attempt a question paper consisting mainly of multiple-choice questions. The sample questions provided by the examination board as part of the 'National

Item Bank' have been found by the schools to be very useful. A very recent development has occurred in some local authority districts whereby a co-ordinated attempt is being made to assist schools in their assessment of pupils following the new materials for the Integrated Science course.

Future Developments in Assessment in Science

It is convenient to consider future developments in assessment of two distinct kinds. The first kind which is considered is the assessment of certain aspects of courses, which is not, at present, included in certificate examinations. The second kind is concerned more with an alternative approach to assessment.

Extension of Assessment in Science

It seems rather ironic, at least at first sight, that in spite of the emphasis placed on pupil experimental work in the new science courses, no formal assessment of practical skills is made in examinations, on either the Ordinary or Higher Grade, in science subjects. Practical examinations were more common, moreover, in traditional science courses, and were held in Scotland until 1955. The aims of experimental work in new courses, however, are quite different from those in traditional courses, and are concerned, mainly, with assisting pupils to discover concepts and relationships, and to practise an enquiry approach in science. Unfortunately, such aims exacerbate the problem of designing appropriate examinations since not only manual skills are involved but also high level intellectual skills.

During a recent investigation, concerned with science subjects on the Ordinary Grade (SCEEB, 1978), two schemes for the assessment of practical work have been studied. The particular abilities which were being assessed were reduced, from the long list of those specified for the courses, to a list of ten in the first scheme, and of four for the second scheme, on the grounds of feasibility. The four abilities were those associated with following instructions, manipulative skill, skill in observing and recording, and interpretative skill. It was concluded that, in spite of the limited range of skills included, neither scheme was completely feasible but that the basis of either could be useful in devising an alternative approach. The principal problem appeared to be that teachers were unable to make judgements on their pupils' practical work in the short time available during a normal class period. No problems were reported, however, in connection with operating either scheme on a national basis. In view of the difficulty which teachers experienced in judging the more basic skills involved in practical work, it would seem unlikely that the schemes investigated would enable assessments to be made of pupils' abilities in formulating and evaluating hypotheses, and in pursuing new problems in the laboratory.

Although a practical examination is not included in the present science examinations for the Ordinary and Higher Grade, a great emphasis is placed on experimental projects in the Certificate of Sixth Year Studies. During these courses, pupils are encouraged to acquire independence in their working, and to practise scientific enquiry for an extended period. It is perhaps unfortunate that a greater number of pupils are not able to benefit from the experience of undertaking a project of this type. Project work is, nevertheless, a common feature in both primary and tertiary education.

116

A particularly difficult area in assessment is that of assessing attitudes. Techniques which have been employed in science subjects range from attitude scales (Brown, 1975; Harlen, Darwin and Murphy, 1977; Kellington and Mitchell, 1978), to methods relying on teachers' use of checklists which list behaviours to be expected of pupils, as they begin to achieve stated attitudes. Certain attitudes, such as objectivity in observation and an objective attitude towards experimental evidence, are clearly important for pupils following science courses. Other attitudes, such as those associated with an awareness of relationships between scientific investigations, or applications of science and the life of society, may become more important in courses presently being developed. It is questionable, however, whether an assessment of attitudes is relevant to certification, although it is undoubtably relevant in the development and evaluation of courses.

A relatively new development in research is that based on cognitive preference testing (Heath, 1964). Such tests are designed to assess what pupils actually do, in an intellectual sense, with information and skills acquired from a course. These tests contrast with normal achievement tests which are concerned, primarily, with assessing what pupils are able to do after following a course. One application of cognitive preference testing to new science courses, is in investigations concerned with the way in which a teacher attempts to guide pupils in their thinking about science by presenting material in a particular manner. Results of such investigations may produce valuable conclusions for use in developing or modifying science courses.

An Alternative Approach to Assessment in Science

The following five statements indicate some of the main problems and limitations of current assessment procedures in science:

1. The listing of candidates in an order of merit is often regarded as the sole function of assessment. As a result, tests are often contrived to produce a wide distribution of scores;

2. Although assessment is considered to be an important part of a science course, particularly in courses leading to certification, it is usually relegated to a time which occurs after the corresponding coursework has been completed;

3. Difficulty has been found in devising forms of assessment which reflect the aims and philosophy of current science courses;

4. Certificate examinations are based on syllabuses which are not sufficiently precise to give a clear specification of expected pupil attainment. As a consequence, the study of previous examination papers and 'teaching for examinations' are common modes of teaching;

5. Except for pupils in S1 and S2, assessment is concerned chiefly with pupils of above average abilities.

The first two statements are concerned with the function of assessment in science which is often regarded solely as a process through which pupils may be listed, in a rank order, to indicate their relative attainment. Assessment procedures can be devised to fulfil other valuable functions, however, and are worthy of further investigation and development. A recent report (*Dunning:* 38), for example, refers to the value of diagnostic assessment in 'providing information on the extent of progress made' and in helping to 'diagnose the difficulties' experienced by pupils 'in order to remedy the situation'. Unfortunately, diagnostic assessment is likely to be difficult to establish, and service, as recognised in the report (*Dunning:* 23). It may well be possible, however, to include diagnostic assessment within an assessment system which could also fulfil other functions.

A useful starting point for such a system of assessment would be the aim to reward all pupils for successful achievement during a course, without consideration of their general abilities, and the extent of achievement of other pupils. It would be desirable to design the system so that information could be obtained to assist in the guidance of pupils through a course, and in the selection of subsequent courses. If the system could fulfil, in addition, the function of providing awards at the end of a course, it would provide a co-ordinated approach to assessment which would link the processes of diagnosis, prognosis and certification whilst rewarding all pupils for successful achievement.

It is very unlikely, however, that a suitable system could be devised on the basis of current science syllabuses which, as indicated in the fourth statement, lack the necessary precision in the specification of expected pupil achievement. The key to the design of an assessment system which could fulfil the above functions is a careful consideration, by course designers and teachers, of the achievement to be expected of pupils who are likely to follow a course. With adequate specifications of expected achievement, the performance of each pupil following a course could be rated, in terms of these specifications. Such specifications are often called 'criteria', and sometimes take the form of educational objectives (Popham, 1978).

This approach to assessment differs, fundamentally, from the procedures which currently are employed. It entails the declaration to pupils and teachers of the level of achievement to be expected in each topic included in a course, and the specification of ways in which pupils are expected to be able to demonstrate their achievement. It could be argued, however, that the statement of such specifications should be the duty of all course designers and examiners since it would avoid, at least to some extent, the undesirable features of teaching, described in the fourth statement. The approach entails, also, the design of assessment procedures which enable all pupils who can demonstrate the required achievement, to be rewarded accordingly, irrespective of their general ability, and the extent of achievement of other pupils.

In order to produce diagnostic information for an individual pupil from a system of this kind, lists of specifications, which the pupil had found difficulty in reaching, would be required. Such information could be obtained through the use of questions suitably indexed in terms of the specifications.

In order to produce prognostic information, a similar procedure to that for diagnostic information could be employed. If the information was required for guiding pupils in their choice of subsequent courses, it would be appropriate to estimate their ability to carry out tasks which would be required on such courses. It might be relevant to estimate, for example, their ability to apply knowledge gained from several activities to the solution of a new problem. If the information is required for guiding pupils in their choice of a career, ability to communicate or to manipulate apparatus might be relevant.

In order to produce information for awards at the end of a course, a number of alternative procedures are possible. Pupils could be assessed, for example, in terms of a random sample of specifications for the course. Alternatively, each specification to be included could be selected as being representative of important groups of specifications. In either case, candidates could be listed in a rank order, in terms of the number of specifications which they had reached, from which awards could be determined. Although this could be preferable to current practice, both of these procedures would not take full advantage of the greater precision in specifications of expected achievement, and in question construction, which should be available.

A procedure for determining awards could be devised, however, in which pupils would be required to display acquisition of specified knowledge, and a specified level of competence in certain skills, in order to obtain a particular class of award. This would ease the problem of attempting to include pupils from a wide range of ability in the same assessment system. It would also enable schools to participate in the process since they could be made responsible for assessing achievement of particular skills. A procedure of this kind would have an advantage over current procedures, which indicate relative levels of achievement on a sample of course content and important skills, since it would allow the linking of awards in national examinations to levels of competence in specified aspects of a course.

Practical Implications of the Alternative Approach to Assessment in Science

The establishment of a co-ordinated system of assessment of this kind would require a detailed specification of expected achievement and appropriate techniques of assessing whether candidates had realised the expectations. It also would require assessment materials to be made available for schools in such a way that they could be used conveniently in the classroom. In addition, assistance in the processing of data, linked with appropriate feedback of information for pupils, teachers and parents, would be highly desirable.

Specifications of expected achievement from each section of the Ordinary Grade syllabus in physics (*Objectives for Ordinary Grade Physics*, Dundee Curriculum Service) were produced in 1977. These form a useful resource for teachers, in their presentation of the course, but are not sufficiently specific for assessment purposes. They would form a convenient basis, however, for the development of a suitable set of specifications. A more suitable set of specifications for the Integrated Science course is included in the teachers' guides (New Science Worksheets Teachers' Guide 1978), for the new materials. These specifications are called 'expected outcomes' and are in the form of behavioural objectives (Vargas, 1972).

The construction of questions which are appropriate for a wide ability range is not easy. An account (Kellington, 1978), is available, however, of the problems and of an attempt to solve them in the case of the Integrated Science course. Particular emphasis is placed in this account on the choice of appropriate vocabulary and language construction. This account also includes a description of an assessment system of the kind being considered which is currently on trial in several schools.

119

Conclusions

Assessment is more difficult for current courses in science than for traditional courses. This is mainly on account of the wider range of intellectual and practical skills which pupils are now expected to acquire. Formal assessment procedures, which can have a substantial influence on the presentation of courses, have begun only recently to include assessment of some of the important skills associated with scientific enquiry. Further progress is likely to be inhibited, however, by the style and content of current science syllabuses.

An alternative approach to assessment, involving the use of detailed specifications of the achievement expected of pupils, offers the possibility of a substantial improvement. Among the advantages of this alternative approach is that assessment could be seen by pupils as an integral part of a course which rewards them for achievement, even if limited, and provides information for guidance when decisions affecting further study have to be taken. An assessment system, based on this approach, could be sufficiently flexible to allow participation by schools in certification, and could encourage the use of diagnostic assessment which could be of considerable benefit to pupils of all abilities. The two greatest benefits, however, would be, firstly, the availability to teachers and pupils of detailed specifications of the achievement expected of pupils and, secondly, the linking of results from assessment procedures to pupils' success in reaching these specifications. These would offer a new opportunity for communicating the philosophy of current science courses, and for encouraging pupils to achieve, more successfully, the stated educational objectives.

References

Assessment for All. Report of the Committee to Review Assessment in the Third and Fourth Years of Secondary Education in Scotland. Edinburgh: HMSO, 1977. 64.

Ausubel, O. P. *Educational Psychology, a cognitive view*. New York: Winston, 1968. 467–504.

Brown, S. A. *Attitude Goals in Secondary School Science*. Stirling Education Monograph No. 1. Stirling: Stirling University, 1975.

Curriculum Paper 7. *Science for General Education*. Produced by the Consultative Committee on the Curriculum, Scottish Education Department. Edinburgh: HMSO.

Harlen, W., Darwin, A. and Murphy, M. *Match and Mismatch: Raising Questions, Match and Mismatch: Finding Answers*. Edinburgh: Oliver and Boyd, 1977.

Heath, R. W. Curriculum, cognition and educational measurement. *Educational and Psychological Measurement*, 1964, *24*, 239–53.

Houston, J. G. *The Principles of Objective Testing in Physics*. London: Heinemann Educational Books, 1970.

Kellington, S. H. *Assessment in Integrated Science—a criterion-referenced approach*. London: Heinemann Educational, 1979.

Kellington, S. H. and McFarlane, I. A. *Assessment in Science in S1 and S2*. Report of project No. H/138/1. Edinburgh: Scottish Education Department.

Kellington, S. H. and Mitchell, A. C. *An evaluation of New Science Worksheets for Scottish Integrated Science*. London: Heinemann Educational, 1978. 91–103.

Klopfer, L. E. *Handbook on formative and summative evaluation of student learning*. Bloom, B. S., Hastings, J. T. and Madaus, G. F. (Eds.). New York: McGraw-Hill, 1971. 559–565.

Lockard, D. J. *The Tenth Report of the International Clearinghouse on Science and Mathematics Curricular Developments*. University of Maryland, 1977.

Nedelsky, L. *Science Teaching and Testing*. New York: Harcourt, Brace and World, 1965.

New Science Worksheets Teachers' Guide, Sections 1 to 8; Teachers' Guide, Sections 9 to 15. London: Heinemann Educational, 1978.

Nuffield O-level Biology, Chemistry and Physics. London: Longmans.

Objectives for Ordinary Grade Physics, Memorandum No. 31. Dundee: Scottish Curriculum Development Service—Dundee Centre, 1977.

Popham, W. J. *Criterion-referenced measurement*. Eglewood Cliffs, New Jersey: Prentice-Hall, 1978.

Report on the Assessment of Practical Work in Science Subjects on the Ordinary Grade. Edinburgh: Scottish Certificate of Education Examination Board, 1978.

Rogers, E. M. *Physics for the Inquiring Mind*. London: Oxford University Press, 1960.

Syllabuses for biology, chemistry and physics on the Ordinary and Higher Grades of the Scottish Certificate of Education. Edinburgh: Scottish Certificate of Education Examination Board.

Vargas, J. S. *Writing worthwhile behavioral objectives*. Chicago: Rand McNally, 1972.

ASSESSING THE SOCIAL SUBJECTS

The social subjects were chosen as a case study because of the problems in assessing the vast area of knowledge covered and the common use of essay type and open ended questions. It is often suspected that the marking of such questions must leave so much to the subjective judgement of the marker that it cannot be reliable. There is evidence to suggest that this is not so, and that markers in History, however subjective they may appear to be, achieve considerable consistency in marking both between scripts for each marker and for the same scripts with different markers.

Bart McGettrick was, before his appointment as an Assistant Principal of Notre Dame College, the evaluator attached to the Curriculum Development Centre at Jordanhill. He is therefore well qualified to provide this review. He has posed the problems associated with assessing the social subjects both as separate subjects and as integrated studies. He highlights the problems occasioned by the wide variety of skills and knowledge involved in dealing with such symbiotic subjects as History or Modern Studies and comes down on the side of using a portfolio of assessment techniques each suited to one or more of the aspects involved.

A.W.J.

Assessing the Social Subjects

B. J. McGettrick

Contents

1. Introduction

Three recent published reports have a profound effect on thinking in assessing the Social Subjects in secondary schools in Scotland, viz., *The Social Subjects in Secondary Schools* (Curriculum Paper 15), 'Assessment for All' (The Dunning Report), and *The Structure of the Curriculum in the Third and Fourth Years of the Scottish Secondary School* (The Munn Report). These publications together offer a view of the nature and place of the Social Subjects in the secondary school, and of a suggested system for assessing them at the end of fourth year of the secondary school. This paper will take account of the general philosophy of those reports and will consider aspects of assessment in the Social Subjects within this broader context.

At the outset it is important to draw attention to the clearly stated case in Curriculum Paper 15, and accepted by the Munn Committee that the generic title of 'Social Subjects' disguises many of the significant differences which exist in the nature of each of the constituent subjects, and that while there may be many similarities these differences cannot be ignored. There are a number of fairly fundamental issues which these reports raise, and which highlight the fact that assessment must be directly related to the philosophy of the curriculum and therefore the whole design of the assessment must reflect not only the content of a subject but the purpose of its place in the curriculum.

Even at the risk of appearing superficial, it is essential to indicate that any issue of assessment is a secondary one. That is, assessment is always related to some more important consideration and in education that is either or both of the curriculum or the pupil. Generally speaking, assessment can be thought of as the activity of providing or collecting information so that an informed decision might be made about something or somebody. In practice it is generally pupils who are thought of as the 'objects' of assessment, but in recent years there has been a recognition that the 'object' might validly be the programme followed by the pupils, teaching methods, teaching materials, and so on. While reference will be made to some of these in this paper, particular attention will be paid to assessment orientated to inform decisions to be made about pupils and their progress. A point worth emphasising is that assessment does not make decisions, it only helps to inform decisions, and therefore the act of making a decision can be seen to be separate from the activity of assessment. This is a significant general point to be considered in any assessment, whether part of a national system or not. Table A lays out schematically the above argument.

(*See Table A page 128*)

Table A

	Purpose of Assessment	Some Likely Characteristics of Assessment
Assessing Pupils	Diagnostic	Internal, Criterion-referenced
	Order of Merit	Internal/external, Norm-referenced
	Certification	External assessment and/or moderation; Criterion-referenced assessment
Assessing Course Outcomes	Appropriateness and value of outcomes	External assessment is useful
	Attainment of specified objectives	Internal/external
	Attainment of other objectives	Internal
Assessing Methods	Efficiency of teaching method	Internal/external

2. Purposes of Assessment

This is clearly not the place to review the range of purposes of assessment, but it is perhaps useful to try to put these purposes into some kind of framework. There is one central or paramount purpose for assessment, viz., providing information so that informed decisions can be taken. One of the most beneficial effects of this statement is the subsequent questions it poses, including: What decisions have to be taken?; Who takes them?; What information will help inform a decision?; How useful is the information collected?; How is assessment data managed?; and so on.

Where pupils are being assessed there are a number of kinds of decisions which can be legitimately influenced by the information gathered. One of the most common uses of assessment information is for diagnostic purposes. If a decision has to be taken as to whether or not a pupil has to move on to another part of a programme may be dependent on being successful at a previous part, this information would most easily be collected by some kind of assessment instrument. Another kind of judgement which may be made, and which involves some form of diagnosis, is deciding if a pupil is in need of particular help in studying a subject. This may be because the pupil has learning difficulties in the particular subject, or because of a more general difficulty in learning. If a pupil has difficulty in dealing with concepts of space or time, these may pose particular difficulties for the Geography or History teacher, although these difficulties are commonly associated with more general problems the pupil faces in learning. A third decision which would benefit from information gathered in assessment is in arranging class groupings. Most forms of groupings are made on the basis of pupil attainment. The groups may be set, streamed, mixed ability, broad banded or whatever, but the basis of their construction is attainment.

For each of these purposes the likely characteristics of assessment are that it would be internal, and, where possible, criterion-referenced. Assessment for diagnostic purposes is, for the most part, likely to be internal. Diagnosis also pre-supposes that reference can be made to some standard or criterion, and so assessment should be criterion-referenced. In practise teachers will require considerable help if criterion-referencing as a common place means of testing is to be implemented, and it might be noted that this help will be necessary not only in test construction, but also in test analysis.

A second major reason for assessing pupils is to establish an order of merit among them. This is again a legitimate educational practice, though perhaps one which has been overplayed in the past, and to little effect. Nonetheless, if an order of merit is to be established it can be achieved by use of either internal or external examining procedures, and the type of assessment should emphasise the range of characteristics or abilities being assessed, *i.e.* a norm-referenced assessment procedure would be designed.

A third major area of concern in orientating assessment to pupils is in the certification of pupils. This is perhaps most commonly encountered in a national assessment system. There are a large number of factors which will affect the nature and type of assessment in the Social Subjects within a national assessment scheme. In such a system there exists a wide range of possible approaches to assessment, but characteristically there would be expected to be some form of external assessment or external moderation of assessment procedures, and there would ideally be a move towards criterion-referenced assessment. While neither of these characteristics are absolutely essential, it would be desirable if they were present if some form of certification or licensing is involved. The arguments for such a system are well set out in *Assessment for All* (The Dunning Report).

Teachers and others involved in testing in its different guises have built up within the profession a wealth of knowledge and experience in assessing more able pupils for certification. This is certainly valuable but it is perhaps limited in terms of the age group involved, particularly in terms of the ability range involved, and also in terms of the rather restricted cognitive area which is traditionally assessed externally. The justification for the existence of the Social Subjects in a school curriculum is not wholly because of knowledge or understanding of cognitive content, and it seems likely that an awareness of this link with the curriculum will have an impact in widening the scope of content of the assessment, the nature of the style of assessment, and the range of ability of pupils being considered for certification.

It would be inappropriate to neglect the assessment of the outcomes of courses, or of the methods used to achieve these outcomes in a discussion of assessment in the Social Subjects. Rather than consider these in detail, however, attention is drawn to Table B (see page 132) which sketches some of the likely characteristics of assessment in these areas when practised in schools. Forms of summative and formative evaluation could be listed in detail, but this would not serve a useful purpose in this paper, especially since most techniques relate to evaluation by a person outwith the teaching/learning environment. Where teachers do become involved in course and pedagogic assessment, usually data is acquired by internal assessment using criterion-referenced measuring techniques. Appropriate external data including external tests or inspections can help to improve the reliability of the internal data, but it may risk having a low validity for the purposes of course evaluation. It is premature to expect widespread development of these approaches, although there is a growing awareness of the possibilities and value of this orientation of assessment. With the development of item banks and criterion-referenced assessment, teachers may well see the value in using information for these purposes. It should be made clear that the technical developments in analysing test information has reached a stage where it is possible to produce item banks and guidance on criterion-referenced tests in the Social Subjects, and the main problem in practice is in teachers' education and awareness. It would certainly be desirable to consider developments in this area despite the implications for resource allocation, in-service training and administration.

3. Assessment and the Curriculum

a. *Assessment in the Social Subjects*

One of the most frequently used models for assessment is the aims and objectives model. Essentially this consists of defining the aims of a subject or subject area, translating these into objectives which are more closely defined, and then finding out if these have been achieved by pupils. This is a fairly straightforward, rational approach to both curriculum design and to assessment. It is clear, explicit and easily understood. Yet it is not without its critics who would claim, among other things, that it is simplistic, mechanical and avoids the complexities intrinsic in the nature of subjects learning and curricular design. It does, however, produce a useful starting point for considering assessment in the Social Subjects, perhaps particularly since the aims and objectives in the teaching of the Social Subjects in the Scottish Secondary school are made so explicit in Curriculum Paper 15.

Having suggested that an 'aims and objectives' model of designing programmes of work in the Social Subjects is possible, it is by no means the case that there would be unanimity, that the stated aims would be agreed by everyone. Indeed there would even be a division of opinion on how best the aims can be defined, for example a subject content approach could be adopted, or, alternatively, a skills or techniques-based approach. While these are not necessarily exclusive approaches they do tend to lay emphasis on different aspects of the subject and this would probably be reflected in the kind of assessment system which would be adopted. Other bases of approach could also be suggested.

b. *The effect of a national approach to curriculum design on assessment*

Having indicated that in the Social Subjects there are a number of approaches to curriculum design it will be apparent that differences at this stage will be reflected in differences in assessment design.

Curriculum Paper 15 offers examples of how aims and objectives of individual Social Subjects can be translated from general statements to fairly specific objectives and thereafter into curricular terms which can be assessed at a number of levels and with different degrees of difficulty. There is no need for the further development of that thinking in this paper.

Rather than take this essentially content orientated approach to the matter of assessment it would be possible to begin by setting out of a classification or taxonomy of objectives such as that proposed by Bloom and others. While such a taxonomy can be applied to any subject or group of subjects, it can also be adapted or developed to apply specifically to one area of interest. An example of how this may be attempted in the Social Subjects is shown in Table B. This table gives a notional framework for constructing tests in the Social Subjects on very broad lines.

One of the advantages in setting out an organised framework such as this is that it draws attention to a number of areas which can be assessed within a subject area or a programme of work. In setting out a grid like this there is a clear articulation of the principal areas of concern within the curriculum and/or, in assessment. These can be stated in terms of content, skills, concepts, processes, or any other way. In designing the assessment it is possible to seek the appropriate balance of items which

Table B

Notional Framework for Test Construction and Assessment in The Social Subjects

	Area to be assessed. Terminology of the subject	NATURE OF TEST ITEM			
		Presence or absence	Internal or external	Recall, application etc.	Type of test item
KNOWLEDGE	Past events and their significance on present situations				
	Significant documents relating to an event, place, or situation				
	The way of life of societies at different times and in different places				
	Factors affecting the way of life of peoples				
	Relationships between events				
	Relationships between physical environment and man's response to it				
SKILLS	**WRITING DESCRIPTIONS**				
	Enquiry—using basic techniques of a subject (*e.g.* by use of sources, map-reading, statistical techniques)				
	Analysis and interpretation				
	Reconstruction and synthesis				
	Judgement				
APPLICATION	Using previous events/or other situations to interpret, reconstruct or judge another event or situation				
	Causality				
	Applying models to new situations				
ATTITUDES	Open-mindedness				
	Empathy				
	Responsibility to society				

will reflect the aims of the curriculum, and to devise items which will be valid. The use of a grid system will bring to mind the various possible components to be assessed and these may include attitudinal factors. It therefore provides a useful conceptual analysis of the assessment of a course and illustrates how it might relate to the aims and structure of the course.

It should be clear of course that Table B gives only an example of the kind of grid which might be formed in assessing the Social Subjects. There are those who would take the view that the Social Subjects are best thought of, and best taught as a group of fairly independent subjects which would include Geography, History, Economics, Economic History and Modern Studies, and may also include Politics, Psychology, Sociology and so on. If one does take this view then the elements of a grid would probably look rather different from those illustrated, though the idea behind its construction would be the same. There would probably be much more detail of content, skills, techniques and principles which would be central to the nature of each subject.

In many respects it is easier to consider the assessment of each of the Social Subjects independently than treating them as a grouping with some common elements in them. Taken as a group there are common issues, but one of the most contentious issues which arises in assessing the Social Subjects is in the assessment of an integrated approach to this area of the curriculum. This raises matters of the responsibility for assessment, the degree of expertise required in teaching integrated courses, the balance of assessment data in these courses, and so on. There is, however, no intrinsic problem for assessment which arises directly from the process of integration in a course, but this approach to curriculum organisation does seem to bring to the fore many of these issues. The kinds of issues which emerge in terms of assessment for the most part are related to the philosophical basis of integration in the curriculum.

A further issue which is frequently related to that of integration, but which is of more general concern is that of attaining a balance within the design of assessment in the Social Subjects. The idea of balance in this respect revolves around validity in assessment and is related to the aims of the course to which the assessment is related, and to the aims of assessment itself.

To achieve balance in terms of the aims of the course is not particularly easy and there is no recipe which can be used to ensure it. The use of a grid as described earlier is perhaps the kind of device which should at least prevent total imbalance in the design in terms of, say, the content of tests or in terms of the style of test used. In using a grid system to help in planning an assessment schedule, it should be clear that balance is not necessarily achieved by all squares in that grid being filled. One of the important issues for the test designer is to be aware of the most important areas to be assessed and to adjust assessment procedures accordingly. A serious shortcoming of a grid system is that these emphases are not made explicit.

In designing assessment it is also important to seek balance in terms of the nature or form of information being received. This really means that close attention should be paid to the purposes of assessment as outlined in the previous section.

4. Techniques of Testing in Assessment

a. *Assessment Design in the Social Subjects*

In considering the most appropriate techniques of assessment to be used in the Social Subjects, it is clear that although there exists a wide range of means of assessment, there are some techniques which are more appropriate for some purposes than others. It is always useful therefore to resort to first principles when selecting the most appropriate assessment technique, and that will involve being aware of what decisions have to be taken and what information will help in taking them. This raises the fairly crucial issue of the distinction between assessment and testing, since testing is only one way of gathering information. In this section particular attention will be paid to testing, the most common form of assessment in schools.

It is glib and a little simplistic to claim that the testing procedures used in the Social Subjects should be related to the teaching of those subjects. This is really only saying that testing should serve the curriculum, and the curriculum is paramount. The assessment procedures adopted are influenced by the curriculum and the decisions which are to be taken. It is important to plan the kind of procedures most appropriate for these purposes, and it is likely that no one single technique will be adequate on its own. In the Social Subjects the range of skills, ideas and concepts encompassed with the subject areas makes it improbable that one approach to testing would be satisfactory for all purposes. For example, even at a very general level it seems obvious that one style of test could be used to assess the kinds of areas indicated in Table B in the previous section.

When designing a system for assessment in the Social Subjects a large number of issues are likely to cause difficulties. For example, there is the matter of the extent to which testing in, say, History is a test of literacy skills, or aspects of assessing Geography testing numerical computation. While there may be legitimate factors which will occur in a testing system their presence need not be such as to render tests invalid. The expertise of the subject teacher needs to be highly developed in setting valid and reliable means of assessment in his subject area, otherwise the influences of external factors can be so great as to render the information gathered from testing worthless.

It is obvious that different decisions to be taken about pupils can be enlightened or informed by different kinds of data. There is no one technique of assessment or testing that is likely to be appropriate for all pupils or for gathering every kind of information which might be required. Indeed a criticism of current practice in the Social Subjects in this regard is that there is not a sufficiently wide range of techniques used by teachers or by examining agencies. There exists in the Social Subjects a form of stereotyping into methods such as essays at one extreme, and multiple choice items at the other. Even where more than one technique is used in an examination or test, the reasons for the choice of the particular technique are often not clear.

In considering the range of techniques available for constructing tests, it seems desirable to encourage teachers to work towards greater variety in their approach to assessment. Some ingenuity as well as time and resources will be needed to be exerted in devising methods of assessment which are not only novel, but also more valid and reliable, less painful, and more direct. This should not be interpreted as a plea for more objective forms of assessment, since the objective/subjective issue is a distraction from the central issues of validity and reliability. In practice this may lead to the development of a 'folio' form or style of assessment in which the folio may include dissertations, essays, objective test data, displays, tape recordings, as well as information gathered through continuous assessment during a course. The diversity of skills, techniques, ideas, concepts and knowledge in the Social Subjects would reinforce the idea of the need to look towards diversity of approaches to assessment and the efficacious use of data gathered.

b. *Some Common Styles of Testing*

There are basically two styles of test item viz., 'free-response' items, and 'structured-response' items, and within each of these styles there exists a fairly large number of variations in kinds of item. This division draws the distinction between items for which pupils themselves have to compose the response and those in which they have to choose the correct response from among a number offered. Clearly this marked difference in type of item in a test is crucial when choosing the appropriateness of kinds of tests for specific purposes. This is vital in the Social Subjects where, on occasions, pupils would be expected to compose a response and indicate an ability to compose logically connected thought, while on other occasions pupils are being tested for facts, understanding or some other more limited objective which may be more validly assessed by structured-response items.

It would not be profitable or desirable to try to describe the main characteristics of 'free-response' and 'structured' response items, but some very general points are made about them in Table C. This needs little comment other than to indicate that in assessment in the Social Subjects free-response items, and principally 'essay-type' assessment (including dissertations) would be of value in considering the ability of a pupil to describe places or events, as well as his powers of analysis, presentation of balanced arguments, demonstration of his degree of empathy and so on. It would be too generalised to think of this form of assessment as more relevant to 'higher order' thinking in the Social Subjects, whereas structured response items may be of greater value in assessing knowledge and elementary understanding, yet this may be a useful way in which to start thinking of assessing in the Social Subjects. As previously mentioned the dangers of producing imbalanced tests are serious and certainly the suggestion here is not that, say, in primary schools, or S1 and S2, pupils are faced with a daunting set of objective test items, which incidentally may cause as great problems in reading as essay items would in writing, and beyond S2 essay items become predominant. At all stages the test designer must be aware of the objectives of the curriculum and be able to relate test items to such objectives. This is as true of external assessment procedures as it is of internal ones, and only where the balance of types, aims or objectives of an external syllabus differs from that of an internal syllabus can a difference in types of test item be expected.

It is frequently claimed by teachers that the serious disadvantage in using structured response items, and in particular multiple choice items, is the time taken in constructing 'good' items. While it is true that it can be a time-consuming task it is possible for the experienced test designer to take short cuts in producing good items, *e.g.*, using frequently quoted wrong answers to open ended questions as distractors in multiple-choice items. What is often forgotten in this argument is the

Table C

Some Common Techniques of Testing in the Social Subjects Types and Relevance

Type	Age Group	Internal/External	Validity/Reliability	Administration	Comment
1. Free Response a. Essay	All ages—though more valid at 12+ (competent writers)	Both, mainly external	Validity—medium Reliability—low	Easily set. Difficult to mark reliably	Danger of literacy competence obscuring competence in the Social Subject. An over-used technique
b. Restricted Response (item completion)	All ages	Mainly internal	Validity—high Reliability—medium	Moderately difficult to set. Generally easily marked and reliable	Need for very accurate, unambiguous phrasing. Response can vary in completeness and this can cause marking problems
2. Structured Response a. Multiple Choice	All ages, but should be competent readers	Both	Validity for certain types of item is high	Can be difficult to set	These techniques are very useful for testing the range of a programme of work. Danger in contriving items once beyond the level of 'understanding' in Bloom's Taxonomy.
b. Matching Items	All ages. More valid at 12+ (competent reader)	Mainly internal			
c. True/false	All ages	Mainly internal	Reliability is high	Easy to mark	With True/false items guessing can pose problems

time taken in construction and marking of free-response items, which when taken conscientiously can far exceed the time taken by using multiple-choice items. This issue should of course, never, or at least only in exceptional circumstances, resolve itself to a question of timing or efficiency. If a test designer thinks through his task then the aims of a course, the methods of teaching, the assumed levels and abilities of pupils, the decisions to be taken at the end of the assessment and the characteristics of types of test item will hold more sway than practicalities of timing and convenience. Again it might be emphasised that in all forms of assessment the validity and reliability of test items is of prime importance.

There is a tendency in the teaching profession to look at issues other than validity and reliability, for example, the apparently endless striving for objectivity in preference to subjectivity. Within the Social Subjects, as elsewhere, this is increasingly recognised as a false god, and less honour is being paid to it. Even in a system where there is large scale national assessment objectivity would not be a desirable end to be pursued for its own sake.

In analysing the validity and reliability of assessment in the Social Subjects a perennial problem is that of assessment in the affective domain. Without trying to skate over the issues which arise in this area it should be suggested that the distinction between the cognitive and affective (and for that matter the psychomotor) domains is a conceptual one rather than one of real practical significance. We are perhaps conditioned to a reductionist view of the curriculum in the Social Subjects, and this may unnecessarily highlight this distinction. Although what has already been said may be seen to relate more to the cognitive than to the affective domain, much of it has relevance for both. It is undoubtedly true that techniques of testing in the affective domain can be viewed with suspicion and even resentment, but even where they are attempted in schools the techniques used are generally poorly developed. There are a number of reasons for this, not the least of which is that teachers in the Social Subjects would have difficulty in arriving at a concensus view of the desirable aims of the Social Subjects within the affective domain. This also raises the thorny issue of the purposes of assessing attitudes and values, and while education may be thought of in some ways as a form of 'social engineering' there is a natural, and, perhaps, healthy reluctance to become too closely associated with such an accusation.

Having said that, there is an equally healthy awareness that the Social Subjects are concerned with aspects of intellectual activity which go beyond factual recall, understanding or indeed any purely cognitive activity. In History, for example, the development of empathy with a person or people at different times or situations may be considered to be as much, or more of the substance of History, as for example, knowledge of an event or fact. In Geography, too, it is recognised by many that an aim of the subject should be to make pupils more aware of the environment in which they live, and this may be more valuable than knowledge about soil types or communication indices. Of course the affective domain will be influenced by knowledge and understanding and it is perhaps only a distraction to raise the issue of assessment in this domain at all, except that it is an area of concern for many who are actively involved both in teaching and in assessment.

The main thrust of this brief discussion on the techniques of assessment has been to suggest that in the Social Subjects, as in all other areas of the curriculum, there is no one strategy which suggests itself at the expense of all others. The kind of decisions which will be made with the knowledge of the assessment data; the issue of whether assessment is internal or external; the age, levels, and abilities of the pupils; the aims and objectives of the course; and the technology available will all have an impact on the method of assessment which is adopted. Clearly no one ideal system exists, but it does appear as if a combination of techniques will be desirable in assessing the Social Subjects.

5. Management of Assessment

Throughout this treatment of assessment in the Social Subjects the theme of needing to relate data to decisions has been to the fore. This may highlight a much neglected aspect of assessment—its management. Even the briefest consideration of this will suggest that if the end product of assessment is in forming a decision, then it is as important to see that the information reaches the appropriate people as it is for that information to be useful.

The issues of particular interest in managing assessment in the Social Subjects may arise from the generic nature of some aims of the subjects individually or within a multi-disciplinary programme and the possible involvement of a number of departments in the secondary school in assessment. In common with other subjects in the curriculum the data from assessment will be used outwith subject departments for certain purposes, so that attention needs to be paid to the kind of information available and how it is presented.

The data from assessment may include information about levels of literacy, oracy, or numeracy, as well as more specific reference to attainment in work specifically related to the Social Subjects, and perhaps information about values or attitudes which has been collected. All these are legitimate, and have to be channelled properly. This may mean in a secondary school the selection and direction of data within Social Subject departments, between departments (both receiving and presenting it to departments other than the Social Subjects), to the Guidance system and to administration within the school. There is also the communication of internal and external assessment data to and from the school, to agencies such as examination boards. careers officers or advisers, prospective employers, and, of course, parents.

Again it should be made clear that there is no ideal or standard way of managing assessment data. Different persons at different times in their institutions require different data depending on the decisions they wish to make. No overall system will be suggested here, but a criticism of much current practice involving both internal and external assessment is that its management is weak, and little attention is paid to using data from other subject assessments, although there are always dangers in transferring assessment data across subjects.

It is a matter for those who design both internal and external assessment programmes to ensure that data are handled in an efficient, effective and professional fashion, and that includes making them available to appropriate agencies outwith the school. This comment is relevant to all assessment but may have a particular significance in the Social Subjects as a group.

Some Areas of Particular Concern

In this section brief reference will be made to four issues which seem to merit particular consideration in any discussion of assessment of the Social Subjects in Scotland at the present time. They are selected on the basis of their topical interest rather than as fundamental principles relating to assessment.

a. *Assessing Pupils with Learning Difficulties*

The Dunning Committee Report, The Munn Committee Report, and the Inspectorate Report on *The Education of Pupils with Learning Difficulties* all point to the need for teachers to be rather more concerned with the assessment of pupils at the lower end of the ability range than we have been in the past. The Dunning Report in particular points to the value in formally and systematically assessing pupils at Foundation Level. It seems likely that extending the range of ability of pupils to be assessed in this way will lead to developments in the techniques of assessment used for such pupils, and this will probably see greater use of criterion-referenced tests.

Table D illustrates some of the techniques which might be used more widely, and which would avoid some of the serious problems raised by use of more traditional forms of assessment in the national system. Some advantages, problems and solutions of the various types of test which might be used in assessing Geography are given in a rather cryptic way. Similar illustrations could be used for more historically or politically orientated courses, *e.g.*, by indicating the use of visuals and photographs instead of maps. The main problems of collecting, analysing and recording this kind of data reliably cannot be minimised, but it would seem likely that with experience, teachers will be able to use a variety of such techniques of assessment to advantage. There will always remain the difficulty of assessing attainment by pupils with language inadequacies, and of relating these to conceptual development. This is an area where much work has to be undertaken both at the level of research, and particularly in the education of teachers if they are to be fully involved in assessment of pupils of all abilities.

b. *Direct Assessment*

Within the Social Subjects there has been a considerable and rapid development of a greater variety of techniques of assessment within the past ten years or so, although their adoption in schools has been slow. This may be interpreted as a laudable attempt to devise increasingly sophisticated, and painless, ways of assessing pupils. No criticism can be or should be levelled at such development, but there does seem to be a related danger of applying even more indirect forms of assessment. The kind of indirect assessment being referred to is that which, for example, takes information from the involvement of a pupil in a simulation exercise or a game, or a group activity. There is no reason why reliable data cannot be collected from these sources, but the validity and reliability of such data would have to be carefully examined.

The point of highlighting this issue is the danger which would occur if all assessment information came from such sources. The information is affected by a considerable number of factors which affect the performance of a pupil in any of these situations, and this reflects on the reliability of the data.

It is a worthwhile and revealing exercise for those involved in assessment design to ask 'Given the aims and objectives of the Social Subjects, what are the most direct ways of assessing these?' In the Social Subjects it might then be legitimate to consider the prospect of assessing contributions to the community, involvement in changing the environment, and so on. This would go further than using assessment

Table D

Examples of Techniques of Assessment for Less Academic Pupils

	Advantages	Problems	Solutions
Written Assessment Free Response	Use of own examples Develop ideas as extensively as they can 'Feeling of accomplishment'	Difficulty of writing Misunderstanding of questions Write irrelevancies Do not know how much to write	Short sentences required for answers Tell pupils the number of sentences Use clear, simple verbs Clear question writing
Structured Response	Easily marked No writing required of pupils Use relevant discrimination between items	Large amount of reading required Distractors can be too close Concentration can be protracted	Can use few distractors Clarity and brevity Think of discrimination level
Map Drawing	Pupils can focus on something Easily recorded data No writing required	Knowledge and map drawing can be confused Marking wide-range Difficult to be sure of pupil's grasp of an idea	Use simple maps Have a clear set of criteria for marking Use appropriate maps
Oral Assessment Role Playing	Test can transfer knowledge Motivation can be high No writing by pupil	Difficulty of empathy and sympathy Difficulty of application Difficulty to record information Difficulty of a common test for all pupils	Use simple, common roles Record 'mark' as you go along
Map/Diagram Discussion	Pupils focus on a problem Can choose an unequivocal example Can discuss a problem at length No writing required	Difficult to record data Time consuming Do not have a necessary vocabulary	Record mark as you go along Encourage pupil by simple direction to aspects on map or photograph
General Conversation	Can probe pupil in depth Can turn conversation in any direction	Difficult to record data Linguistic difficulties Shyness Communication by pupil—difficult	Record mark as you go along Put pupil at ease (frequent tests)

from field work or practical work, and would perhaps offer greater opportunities for considering why and how subjects are taught.

c. *Technology and Assessment*

Much of how we think about assessment is influenced by present practice and past experience, but it would be naive and irresponsible not to have an eye to likely technical developments which seem likely to have a profound impact on assessment. We are told that we are on the verge of major social changes with the widespread production and use of silicon chip micro-electronics. The fast falling costs of production and the speed of operation of these devices will have an impact on the nature of the Social Subjects, the way they are taught in schools, and on the assessment of pupils in schools. As yet this development has not seriously affected current practices, nor has it had any effect on the kind of computer potential which has emerged prior to 'the chip revolution'. The revolution is in availability rather than in computer operation.

The increased accessibility to information systems such as 'Prestel' (or 'View Data'), 'Ceefax', 'Oracle' and so on, will surely lead to the establishment of national item banks for assessment. This would encourage the setting up of criterion-referenced assessment in a teaching context of computer-managed teaching and learning. The possibilities for development seem endless, but the previous warnings of avoiding indirect forms of assessment, and its relevant management should be kept in mind.

Perhaps the most significant advantage of the availability of computer potential is in the management of assessment data. Within the Social Subjects it has been pointed out that there is need for a transfer of data among teachers in schools, commonly in different departments in a secondary school, and in offering information outwith the school. The ease with which this could be achieved on casette with readily accessible print-out or viewing facilities makes the prospect of efficient assessment systems more of a reality.

A further warning perhaps. In a world of education with silicon chips over-assessment seems a real danger.

d. *A National System of Assessment—and Conclusion*

As a conclusion to this treatment of assessment in the Social Subjects it is worth considering the prospect of a national programme of assessment which attempts to bring all pupils within its compass. A number of important practical issues arise. Apart from the difficulties which may emerge from the framing of nationally acceptable syllabuses, there are problems of criteria by which gradings will be established, and standards set and maintained.

Within the Social Subjects the very nature and organisation of the subjects are in question. These will differ for different ages and perhaps for different abilities (see Curriculum Paper 15). There must be scope for teacher initiative and flexibility, and this will have an impact on a national system in which there is a balance of internal and external assessment. The development of item banks and forms of criterion-referenced assessment will help fix points of reference in national assessment, and it may be that sampling assessment will allow for a pattern of continuous moderation to be developed.

In such a developing system it will be crucial to establish a framework for staff development. Whether this is done through setting up some formal agency or by using in-service facilities as they currently exist, it will be necessary to ensure the continuing up-dating of staff of pupils at all ages and of all levels over a range of issues on assessment, so that education will benefit from the efforts put into this operation.

References

Assessment for All. Report of the Committee to Review Assessment in the Third and Fourth Years of Secondary Education in Scotland. SED, HMSO, 1977. ('The Dunning Report').

Pupils in Profile: Making the most of Teachers' Knowledge of Pupils. SCRE/HAS, Hodder and Stoughton, Edinburgh, 1977.

The Education of Pupils with Learning Difficulties in Primary and Secondary Schools in Scotland. A Progress Report by HM Inspectors of Schools. SED, HMSO, 1977.

The Social Subjects in Secondary Schools. Curriculum Paper 15. The Scottish Central Committee on Social Subjects, 1976.

The Structure of the Curriculum in the Third and Fourth Years of the Scottish Secondary School. SED, HMSO, 1977. ('The Munn Report').

MUSIC AND ASSESSMENT

'How sour sweet music is when time is broke and no proportion is kept.'

Richard II Vv 42

Said by Richard moments before his death, those lines meant something quite different from the interpretation intended here. Yet there is a sour sweetness about Music in the curriculum when its assessment is as much out of proportion as this paper would suggest.

It is frequently said that the most difficult areas of the curriculum to define in terms of objectives and the most difficult to assess by other than essentially subjective means are those areas in which creativity plays a considerable part. It is claimed by some that the artist is born not made and that while teaching may help to heighten the students' awareness and knowledge of materials which may provide him with techniques he would otherwise lack, yet the work of art which he produces may contravene all the accepted tenets and still be recognisable as a thing of beauty and of lasting value as a creative statement. Indeed the act of creation, it is argued, is itself a crossing of frontiers beyond that which has already been achieved and could not have been anticipated. It is therefore impossible, they say, to determine criteria with which to judge an artefact and therefore to assess in the creative arts except subjectively. The judge, they argue, feels the rightness of the object rather than intellectualises it.

While this is possibly true of Mozart, Menuhin or McDiarmid, yet others argue that we all judge artefacts by certain criteria and that if we can articulate these we can then assess the relative merits of different practitioners in reaching these criteria. Most practitioners at school level, they would argue in any case, are still acquiring necessary skills and it would be reasonable to assess these skills against known norms of performance for age and stage.

A third view is expressed that for most pupils the creative arts are aesthetic experiences rather than any beginning to a training as performer or practitioner, and that what should be assessed, therefore, during compulsory schooling, are the effects which these aesthetic experiences have had on the attitudes of pupils exposed to them.

145

In an attempt to look at how one subject, Music, has faced up to the problems so far, Mr Weir, a music specialist in HM Inspectorate of Schools in Scotland was commissioned to produce this paper. Mr Weir has been concerned for some time about the validity and reliability of much which has passed for assessment in music and has welcomed the opportunity, if not the work involved, to search through the literature and to contrast what is being done with what might be done.

While much has been achieved, both by means of standardised tests of knowledge and by practical tests of the playing of instruments and writing of music, to diagnose to predict and most frequently to grade students likely to become professional musicians, almost nothing has been done to assess effectively the consequence of the musical studies which some 90 per cent pupils in primary and secondary schools are required to undertake. Curriculum Paper 16 'Music in Scottish Schools' has much to say about what should be included in courses for such pupils. The Munn Report has suggested that some creative art should be in the curriculum of all pupils and music is one of the subjects through which this should be achieved. Mr Weir says something about what might be done to assess such work but possibly not enough. What he does say, however, gives us much food for thought and may be sufficient to stimulate the development of suitable techniques for any Dunning type certification which may come to us in the future.

A.W.J.

Music and Assessment

R. S. Weir

'But bright Cecilia raised the wonder higher
When to her organ vocal breath was given,
An Angel heard and straight appeared
Mistaking earth for Heaven'

Dryden

The Angel revealed a lack of:

1. musical talent
2. musical aptitude
3. musical achievement
4. musical training
5. musicality
6. musicianship

Underline the phrase which in your opinion most closely fits the situation. On appeal, how would you judge whether the Angel's mistake was genuine, or an excuse for defection? The Angel might cite Sir Thomas Browne in *Religio Medici:*

'for even that vulgar and tavern musick which makes one man merry, another mad, strikes me in a deep fit of devotion, and a profound contemplation of my Maker'.

A judge could counter with the following dictate from an old Royal College of Music examination paper:

'Attack convincingly one who says "I know little about music, but I know what I like".'

Lack of objective measures is the cause of conflict in this case. The Angel's descent to the fundamental firmament might be considered quite creditable by another judge. On this occasion, however, reference can be made to the Omniscient Authority for the ultimate decision. For mere mortal music makers there is only the judgement of Solomon—as personified in the verdict of the external examiner.

Aptitude

For five decades, research in musical assessment has been concerned mainly with the important but narrow field of testing aptitude. In Scotland, the most frequent references made are to tests by Seashore, Wing, and Bentley. These tests are often used to select pupils for instrumental tuition.

The rationale of aptitude testing has been criticised. Leonhard (1958) came to the conclusion that 'the present state of development of tests of musical capacity does not warrant their use as the whole determinant in screening students'.

In his view the validity of known music tests was 'questionable and confused'.

Part of this confusion is related to the definition of musical talent and the nature of musical abilities. Musicality, musical achievement, musical aptitude, musical attainment, and musical capacity are freely used in differing contexts and just as freely interchanged. At a more mature stage, 'musicianship' is an ill-defined holistic term among music educators.

148

Another cause of dissension is the nature/nurture debate about the respective contributions to musical development of heredity and environment. Wing (1963) subscribed to the belief that aptitude is inborn:

'All that the teacher can do is to provide the right conditions for development of the child's inborn powers'.

Seashore (1938) supported this thesis:

'fortunes have been spent and thousands of young lives made wretched by the application of the theory that the sense of pitch can be improved with training. It is the cause of the outstanding tragedy in musical education'.

Research by McGuire and Associates (1960) contradicts Wing and Seashore: 'talented behaviour is acquired and becomes organised, or structured, and to some extent predictable as a consequence of the educative process'.

Attributes of pitch and rhythmic discrimination, tonal memory, chord analysis, and timbre differentiation are desirable musical qualities. If, however, these fundamental musical characteristics can be improved by training, then 'instant' measures of musical aptitude might be the result of previous musical experience or environmental influences rather than indicators of innate potential. Other important attributes are the ability to learn, to remember, and to perceive. The sensory acuity needed for interpretation requires insights which are non-auditory and non-cognitive. Tests to predict future musical behaviour, therefore, should also take account of cognitive, personality and motor factors which have a bearing on the acquisition of musical skills and the maturing of perceptions.

Phenix (1962) develops the argument further: 'although a knowledge of music theory, including an ability to analyse patterns of rhythm, melody, harmony, and tone colour—the basic elements of all music—may be helpful, such rational competence does not in itself disclose aesthetic meanings'. He also writes: 'Musical understanding is consummated in love'.

There are implications for Scottish music educators. If the auditory powers as designated by Wing, Seashore, Bentley, and others, are untrainable, then for many years much of the skill-based curriculum in Scottish schools has been fallacious. On the other hand, if musical understanding is consummated in love there are many adults and pupils who will testify to the impotence of the traditional class-music lesson.

The temptation to concentrate on qualities and abilities apparently linear in development and easily measured has permeated musical education this century. Universities, conservatoires, and teacher-training establishments emphasised academic and disciplinary aspects of music in a search for academic respectability. As recently as March, 1978, in *Music in Education,* Crickmore, in referring to the Gulbenkian Report on *Training Musicians* emphasised the need to re-integrate music into an overall epistemological system and quoted Lord Vaizey, Chairman of the Committee of Enquiry: '. . . music as a general subject is an intellectual discipline . . . a broadly based musical education, that includes the theory, structure and history of music as well as execution, and above all a degree in music can be just as much a preparation for—say—a civil service or business career as a degree in history or physics is generally accepted to be'. Another aspect of the academic influence was noted by Nunally (1964) who referred to the lack of research into evaluation and measurement of aesthetic attributes and achievements. He believed that this was due to 'practical considerations of the demand for intellectual and vocational tests in academic fields'.

In recent years research has extended towards testing more complex musical phenomena. Expressive, interpretative, and aesthetic dimensions have been more deeply investigated. Work of significance has been completed by Lundin, Farnsworth, Petzold, Meyer Oakes, Gordon Tarrell, Wolfe, Fosha and others in America, Revesz in the Netherlands, and Mainwairing, Rees-Davies, Bentley and others in Britain. In some cases findings are in disagreement, and there has been criticism of conclusions based upon small samples, even when research design and statistical techniques have been correct. There is a strong body of opinion against the use of factorial techniques in musical investigation, but so far there is little evidence of experimentation in the application of research methods from other areas of aesthetics. The influence of these research findings on musical education has been negligible. It is apparent that the design of reliable instruments to measure aptitudes, attitudes, musicianship, and performance requires further experimentation involving longitudinal studies of much larger samples of schools and pupils.

Subjectivity

Colwell (1964) noted an increasing demand for objectivity rather than subjectivity in musical measurement. Fourteen years later, assessment is still greatly dependent on an abundance of subjective evaluation, formal and informal, related to all aspects of musical activity. The following comment by a newspaper's music critic reveals the underlying assumptions in this style of assessment. 'On tour, the traditional formality between performers and critics soon collapses. "How do you preserve your objectivity?" I am sometimes asked when I return from my travels with an orchestra. In fact it is not so difficult. Performers, when they ask your opinion about last night's concert, do not want to be fobbed off with verbal bromides. "How did it really sound?" they will ask' (*Weekend Scotsman* 21.10.78).

This critic is somewhat confused about idealism, realism, subjectivity and objectivity.

The propensity for subjective evaluation is well documented, even in Chaucer: 'Therewith ye have of musicke more feeling than had Boece, or any that can sing'.

This is a very early example of norm-referenced assessment. Chaucer also anticipated the visiting examiner: 'Trewely the cause of my coming was only to herken how ye sing'.

Nye (1963) pointed out that if measurement determines how much has been learned, and evaluation determines the quality of the process, then evaluation is the more important aspect in music as qualitative judgements are a regular feature of subjective assessment. However, judgement of achievement can only be made relative to some standard of progress towards curriculum objectives and modes of assessment are undefined. The exception is the Scottish Certificate of Education syllabus for examinations in music at 'O' and 'H' grades, but recent evidence submitted to the Scottish Certificate of Education Examination Board (SCEEB) indicates disquiet even with this long established system of assessment. It is pertinent to look at some aspects of current national examinations.

The Visiting Examiner

In the SCEEB publication, *Guidance for Teachers on the Setting and Marking of Examinations in Music* (1968), the following statement appears '. . . the Board's Examiners are intent on rewarding a high standard of general musicianship rather than a certain facility in one department. The attainment of such general musicianship is, surely, the goal of both the teacher and the taught'. Under the heading 'Oral and Practical Examinations' marks are allocated thus:

Table I

Oral and Practical Mark Allocation

Subject	O	H
Sight Singing	30	25
Oral Ear Tests	20	15
Professed Pieces	40	30
Viva Voce	5	5
Scales and Arpeggios Sung to solfa	5	—
Scales and Arpeggios	—	10
Sight Reading	20	15
Keyboard Harmony	—	15

The Board's intentions are laudable. Not everyone, however, agrees that the list of items in Table I and the weighting given to each is the best way of defining or measuring the general musicianship which they wish candidates to achieve. This is not helped by the present system of examining.

The visiting examiner in about thirty minutes assesses a pupil's achievements in this range of activities and reports to the Board by means of a brief verbal report and a numerical score. The work assessed is mainly the result of extended study and could come under a heading of General Musicianship. Many teachers argue that the practical examination can only be ephemeral because of the short time available for each candidate and are concerned that the only record of the transaction is the Examiner's report. Appeal is difficult in such circumstances.

In addition, the structure of the examination lends itself to abuse. While the Board surely sees music as a whole, music teachers could, and sometimes do, prepare candidates by requiring them to master the various elements separately, keeping instrumental performance, sight reading, sight singing scales, arpeggios and aural tests in quite water-tight compartments. When this method is used, we almost return to a system of aptitude testing, applying atomistic measures to derive a holistic conclusion. Gestalt theorists have been critical of such methods.

If practical assessment is to be undertaken efficiently it must be considered in relation to:

1. the objectives of musical education;

2. the pupil qualities to be assessed;

3. the means of assessing these qualities;

4. the attributes required by a visiting examiner;

5. inter and intra-examiner reliability, and

6. external and internal assessment.

The Board's present system perhaps pays less attention to the last two of these items than is desirable, since no regular standardising experience appears to be given to examiners, nor are examiners given a random selection of candidates. The advice given to them before they begin is valuable in establishing a common standard for their own candidates, but does little to facilitate later inter-marker standardisation. Subsequent national standardisation is only adequate if each examiner is allocated a group of schools or candidates considered to be a representative sample. This would presuppose that criteria for selection have been decided. Another method of standardising might be to adjust marks according to the known characteristics of the examiner. This method must take account of Helmstadler's (1964) conclusion that reliability of subjective measures is frequently impaired because judges are:

1. too lenient;

2. tend to be influenced by each other;

3. are unable to cope with the complexity of behaviours to be evaluated;

4. are influenced by the 'halo' effect;

5. tend to avoid the use of extreme positions on a rating scale.

It is evident that some at least of the Board's present procedures for oral examining are more open to challenge than should be the case for an examination for external certification, and upon which entry to professional training may depend. Musical experience is an amalgam of skills, knowledge and attitudes. Listening and performing skills, attitudes and appreciations are the most difficult to measure. Some of the difficulties will now be considered.

Aural Skills

The use of atomistic test measures of aural response do not match the aim of cultivating listening skills—enhanced understanding and appreciation of music heard and read, leading to interpretative ability in performance and the capacity to make qualitative judgements, yet because of its specificity a pupil may score high in the present practical examination without being the discriminating musician envisaged.

Macpherson (1923) has used the term Aural Culture. It is in this sense of cultivation and refinement that 'aural training' is of value, not in the sense of responding to contrived examples of intervals, rhythms, chords, cadences, modulations, or whatever, out of any useful musical context.

More emphasis should be given to the structure and sensory effects of melodic and harmonic intervals and chords in works heard, played, and studied. Less time might be given to dictation and more to aural/visual location of pitch and rhythm discrepancies in melodic and harmonic passages. These are experiences which are relevant to individual and group music making. Objective assessment of these skills can be undertaken without the services of a visiting examiner.

Musical taste is abstract and subjective. It is derived from a cultural heritage with established subjective values. Assessment therefore, should be concerned with knowledge and aural/visual capacity to identify and classify musical phenomena, and to differentiate between appropriateness or inappropriateness of interpretation with regard to accuracy, tempo, dynamics, articulation, period, and style. The present SCE alternative O-grade sets an example which could be a basis for development in this field.

There is need for item banking of good tests of aural perception properly pre-tested and categorised. The subjectivity in assessing non-performance musical behaviour could be reduced by providing judges with samples of test scripts illustrating desirable responses. The aim must be to assess by methods which encourage aural cultivation and promote aesthetic response.

Reading

The visiting examiner at present must also assess sight singing and sight reading. Standardising tests for a large number of musical instruments is a task of some magnitude. If such assessment is to continue, banks of approved tests for vocal and instrumental reading should be compiled to ensure as even a standard as possible. A main objective must be to provide examiners with frames of reference based on recorded examples of tests with scores. Any consideration of reading processes should, however, take account of this quotation from Dykema and Cundiff (1939): 'The ability to read music is granted by everyone to be a valuable accomplishment. That this ability opens up a world of enjoyment and produces a stimulating feeling of mastery is not doubted. It is the process of gaining this power and the seeming necessity of the consequent neglect of other valuable phases of musical experience which have caused controversy among music teachers. We are coming to believe now that the problem of sight reading can in itself be musical and interesting, thus strengthening instead of impairing the love of music.'

There is need to weigh the interpretative aspects of sight reading as well as the technical demands for which tests are usually constructed. A variety of short excerpts related to work in aural culture and testing facets of perception such as articulation, phrasing, rhythm, pitch, and dynamics should be produced. There are strong musical arguments for an integrated approach to this activity but the desirable balance between technical and interpretative demands should be carefully explored.

Instrumental Performance

As in music reading, attempts have been made to produce objective tests of performance attainment. At present, only elementary standards are tested and, consequently, assessment of more advanced performance is still subjective and measured only against culturally approved criteria. The concert-goer, music critic, festival adjudicator, and visiting examiner each functions freely within this area.

It is difficult to suggest how the subjective element might be reduced in the short term. Perhaps standards could be established by providing examiners with cassette tapes of sample performances together with a written commentary and an analysis of how the mark was derived. A further development would be to provide an 'unseen' for marking, although factors other than the auditory effect would be missing. The present SCE scale of proficiency, incorporating terms such as 'exceptional' and 'satisfactory' leaves much to be desired.

Many candidates have external instrumental tuition. As a result, some teachers ignore this part of the examination—a further indication of disparate item preparation. If the curriculum is to be based on the premiss that aural/visual concepts, aesthetic awareness, and performance achievement are inter-related, the teacher must accept that music is an integrated study in which performance achievement is a higher order phenomenon. This topic is developed further in the section on affective response.

Harmony, Counterpoint, Creative Composition

There is no more strongly established tradition in music examinations, at all levels, than the testing of Harmony and Counterpoint, and no other examination 'subject' has been so frequently criticised.

The present SCE examinations in Harmony and Counterpoint are based on stylistic imitation. Ideally the candidate will apply aural/visual skills to writing in these forms and become familiar with different idioms through wide experience of the work of appropriate composers. In practice the examination syllabus influences aural teaching in such a way that the mechanics of the process leave little scope for analysis, evaluation, or synthesis.

The weakness of a narrowly stylistic study is that the externalised criteria can be imitated by teaching which is superficial and does not add depth to the pupil's experience. This is also true of the traditional approach to 'Melody Making'. Smith (1947) criticised the constraining effects of external examinations because 'As things are, my candidates are unable to offer for examination their most outstanding work, a quite idiotic state of affairs it seems to me.'

His comment has particular relevance to the relationship between stylistic musical constraints and creative composition. Schools with an open door policy in the music department have interval and lunch-time devotees who become familiar with chords and their progressive effects by exploring a variety of keyboard instruments and guitar. Group improvisation is frequently heard. Pupil arrangements and compositions of interest are sometimes produced and performed, but none of this work is externally examined. It should be.

Assessment of stylistic studies can be objective. Musicality is the more difficult dimension to measure, but it is related to cultural expectations of which examiners are presumably aware. It would be interesting to analyse the effect which errors in part-writing have on the examiner's mark for musicality. Work observed in schools testifies to increasing impatience as the red pencil tracks the consecutives, overlaps, falling leading notes, and all such anathemasa.

Evaluation of creative work, however, presents problems. By definition, a creative piece might have no cultural or stylistic criteria beyond the intention of the composer. To establish examination expectations could encroach on the creative initiative by substituting for stylistic criteria another set of externals. Yet an enterprising teacher will stimulate a talented pupil by offering a wide variety of music for listening and performance; reference will be made to melody, rhythm, timbre, dynamics, instrumentation, harmony, and form; attention will be drawn to the nuances, variety, balance, tension and release; attempts will be made to give the pupil access to insights on the unity and uniqueness of the work. In so doing, the teacher implies the basis of assessment although these implied criteria are much less constraining than the style of Bach for a pupil who lives in the time of Bowie, Berio and Boulez.

Appreciation

Musical appreciation, like musicianship, lacks definition. In teaching towards examinations it is frequently limited to the study of set works. Such study is referred to in an article entitled 'How to Fail an "O" Level and Become an Integrated Personality' by Antony Hopkins in *Living Music* (Autumn 1969). His theme is the sterility of an analytical approach to music, and the frustrating aridity of questions in 'O' and 'A' level examinations. In referring to the effective 'ghost' music passage in Bartok's 'Music for Strings, Percussion, Piano, and Celeste' he gives an example of the analyst's approach:

'The passage between bars 20 and 33 marked *piu andante*, consists of a sustained harmony of the 4 consecutive tones D to A played on muted violins with a trill on each note. Above this, an *ostinato* passage of descending and ascending major 7ths is found as chordal dissonances in the piano and muted glissandi in the 2nd violins. Celeste and two solo violins have a long melodic line above this sustained background, the angular chromatic intervals of which make it difficult to define in terms of tonality.'

Hopkins comments:

'What contribution to human knowledge is really made by writing rubbish like this? I might get my "A" level, but what evidence would I have given of being sensitive to music? . . . What I try to do is increase your understanding, which is not the same thing as knowledge, and with it, the intensity of your response. Now response, understanding and feeling are very difficult to examine in text book terms. . . . Out come the dreary old defensive moves, give the kids some facts that they can trot out—there's a modulation into the dominant in bar 16, 2 marks. Confronted with such mentality, I'm afraid I just want to run away—back to Bartok.'

Earlier, Debussy wrote in similar vein in 'La Revue Blanche': 'Men in general forget that as children they were forbidden to dismember their playthings, but they still will persist in poking their aesthetic noses where they are not wanted.' The answer to the problem lies somewhere between the extreme views of the analyst/examiner and Debussy.

Pickford (1948) undertook research into the aesthetic and technical aspects in artistic appreciation. He concluded that the aesthetic factor combined form and design with emotional expression, and that the technical factor contrasted rhythm, sentimentality and accuracy of representation with impressionism, colourfulness, and symbolism.

The implication is that music of intrinsic value has formal constructs and qualities of expressiveness of a high order. Music educators must consider whether present examinations encourage greater appreciation of all qualities of a composition or, in the words of Hopkins, '. . . many children will relegate Bartok into the category of boring old school work as a result of being forced to dissect every page of the score.'

Robert Witkin (1974) noted this ubiquitous approach to appreciation when observing the use of 'pop' in the classroom: 'One does not usually have to look very far beneath the surface of the music teacher's use of "The Cream", "Led Zeppelin", or "The Grateful Dead" to find the real package. It comes in the form of "unusual rhythmic sequences", "really clever chord progressions", and "complex harmonies". . . . To the pupil this can often seem patronising and strongly irrelevant because it ignores or misconstrues the use that he actually has for pop music.'

Affective Responses

Central to the discussion of 'musical appreciation' is this problem of externalising and assessing affective response. 'In short, the immense value of music to a boy in the education of his emotions which is, indeed, the main purpose of music in a school is not examinable at all, and may only be observable in the greater sensitivity and serenity of his future life.' (Smith, 1947).

Smith's time scale is, however, too extended for the more immediate demands of national examinations.

The effect of a modulation is much more complex than 'bar 16, 2 marks'. The difficulty for the pupil is to communicate how he construes its effect when it may be sub-conscious and beyond his understanding. If, however, aural/visual studies are regarded as experiences which develop cognitive and sensory concepts of qualitative analysis, synthesis, and musical appreciation, the integration of 'set works' and other compositions within these studies is a natural concomitant. It is to be hoped the pupil will acquire an appropriate vocabulary to describe sensory affects and how these are conceptualised and manifested by himself as listener.

The terms 'understanding', 'sensitive', 'perceptive', and 'intuitive' are nebulous but have accepted relevance to musical behaviour. They describe qualities which are desirable attributes in the musically aware. Progress towards assessment of the degree to which these attributes are revealed by behaviour has been slow. Reference has already been made to ways in which criteria derived from social and cultural traditions might set standards, but criterion-referenced testing of musical behaviour at higher levels of concept attainment presents difficulties. Measurement of non-performance aesthetic reactions remains the most complex problem of all.

One manifestation of aesthetic awareness is in performance, but the act of performing is limited by degree of technical proficiency and the intrinsic musicality of the work. But if performance achievement is highly dependent on auditory perceptual ability it might be possible to abstract a hierarchy of perceptions such as those associated with sensation, symbol, figure, meaning, and overall adjustment of performance to externals. It is debatable however whether an external examiner can always differentiate between a performance which is the outcome of drilling and teaching and one which is the result of observation and imagination. Most examiners would probably profess that assessment of the balance between perceptive behaviour and teaching input is not within their remit.

It is evident that the present system of itemised evaluation by visiting examiners is deficient in the quality of tests, mode of administration, lack of standardisation, and the quality of information derived from the short assessment session. If more suitable tests of perceptive abilities and conceptualisation are devised, a great deal of time would be required for administering and scoring. Judges would need training in applying and interpreting the measures. The cost will be very high. Consideration, therefore, must be given to internal and continuous assessment as appropriate means of measurement of musical phenomena.

General

During the past two years the Munn and Dunning reports have been published, Curriculum Paper 16 (*Music in Scottish Schools*) has been distributed, and the SCE examination in music at 'H' grade has come under review. The opportunity to consider methods and techniques of assessment is unprecedented.

The first task must be to arrive at a consensus on the desirable curriculum. No doubt there would be agreement on general principles such as the desirability of developing listening skills, performance skills, compositional skills, and acquiring contextual knowledge, but objectives, content, methodology, and evaluation techniques must also be clearly stated. The present examiners have not related what is assessed against any criteria other than traditionalism. Opportunities to relate kinds of knowledge to each other are missed because of the fragmentary nature of the assessment process. While the cognitive bias does include a practical as well as an intellectual capacity in a narrow sense, the non-cognitive and conative factors which are fundamental to aesthetic experience are only marginally assessed.

The extended period of historical and musical development of which candidates are expected to have knowledge is unrealistic. Methods of teaching this tend to be after the fashion of Lucy in one of Schultz's 'Peanuts' cartoons:

Linus—'I can't memorise something like this in a week, this is going to take research. "Who was Jeremiah? Where was Rama? Why was Rachel so upset?" You can't recite something until you know the Who, the Where, and the Why.'

Lucy —'I'll tell you the Who, the Where, and the Why. You start memorising right now or you'll know Who is going to slug you, and you'll know Where she's going to slug you, and you'll know Why she slugged you.'

There is a definite need to consider the place of contextual knowledge and its relevance to musical studies.

Mention has already been made that the examinations do not allow pupils to 'present their best work'. When consideration is given to the purpose and ability range for which the examinations are intended, further constraints are perceived, mainly due to the practical requirements.

The purpose of the present 'H' grade course appears to be to prepare pupils for a tertiary education in music but 'H' grade music even at the highest award does not ensure entry to a music academy or university. These institutions demand that their own pre-entry requirements are satisfied and 'H' grade is not taken into account except as a general educational requirement. The implication of the 'H' grade examination is that there is a normative scale of musicianship measured on a continuum of one overall ability. This is not necessarily so. Consider the opportunities available at post-school level:

1. The Royal Scottish Academy of Music provides for a wide development in performance and general practical musicianship;

2. Some colleges of education provide a 3-year course with emphasis on school music teaching;

3. Some colleges of education provide a BEd course in music;

4. Universities offer a variety of course from BMus to BA or MA with music as a course credit.

For some of these courses there are few or no practical demands. Courses can be interest-based as in a study of TV and Film music. At tertiary level, therefore, provision is made for pupils across the board, keyed or otherwise.

Examinations do affect teaching programmes, and it is sensible to accept this and try to use it to advantage. If there is a need, and a future, for the informed concert-goer, the performer, the budding composer, the musicologist, the liberal arts students, and improved quality of life for all, opportunity arises for current reviews to design appropriate courses to provide for a variety of interests and specialisms. This can influence all stages of the school.

The Munn proposals are also relevant. Music can offer examinable interest-based courses at various levels of maturity and attainment. Full and short courses can be provided to meet the Dunning proposals, and beyond. The principle of differentiation can be fully exploited on both ability and interest. Content is of marginal importance in this respect.

Linear development has a bearing on the acquisition of technical skills in performing. Other cognitive and affective aspects of music can mature in experiential form. The level of maturity is reflected in the pace of teaching, the depth of learning, and in the performance, motivation, and commitment of the pupil.

The nature of musical experiences provides overlapping flexibility, not so much in relation to content as in relation to the extent of progress towards desired objectives. If provision is made for assignment options it is feasible that a pupil entering the study at Foundation level could complete a task in more than creditable terms. An enthusiasm might be explored in depth. Why not have units of study including research and performance on a group of instruments such as recorder and early wind instruments, music in the Reformation, music and advertising, music and propaganda, film and TV music, the rise of nationalism, the composer and the environment, and music and literature? A performer might play a recital programme on one or more instruments. This task could be related to a study paper on the repertoire professed. A budding composer could sit a paper on stylistic studies and submit a folio of original composition. All submissions could be accompanied by tapes, transparencies and other relevant material. There may be organisational and administrative problems but with internal assessment permitted, these should not be insurmountable.

There are many problems to be solved in finding reliable measures of affective response at mature levels. In practice, the best person to observe and record pupil development is the class teacher. This is the course of action which is invariably recommended when external assessment presents difficulties. In the case of music, however, the recommendation to assess internally is justified. The inherent weaknesses in the system are recognised but these can be remedied by appropriate teacher training. External moderation in some form should remove any remaining doubts.

This paper has argued that there is much wrong with music courses in our schools, and, the ways in which these courses are assessed. Fortunately, music education is at a stage when change is possible and will be fairly readily accepted. The opportunity must be seized to try new things, to conduct research into new methods of assessment and to produce new assessment instruments which will not only be more valid and reliable, but will also help to stimulate new, interesting, and affective teaching for pupils of all musical interests and tastes.

References

Colwell, R. 'An Investigation of Musical Achievement among Public School Students'. _Journal of Educational Research_, 57, March 1964.

Dykema, P. W. and Cundiff, H. M. _New School Music Handbook_. Summy-Birchard Co., Evanston, 1939.

Helmstudler, G. P. _Principles of Psychological Measurement_. Appleton-Century-Crofts, New York, 1964.

Leonhard, C. _Evaluation in Music Education_. NSSE 57th Year Book, 1958.

Macpherson, S. _Melody and Harmony_ Bk 2. Williams, London, 1923.

McGuire, C. and Associates. _Talented Behaviour in Junior High Schools_. Final Report, Project No. 025, The University of Texas, 1960.

Nunnally, J. C. _Educational Measurement and Evaluation_. New York: McGraw-Hill, 1964.

Nye, R. E. _Music for Elementary School Children_. Washington DC, Centre for Applied Research in Education, 1963.

Phenix, P. H. _Realms of Meaning_. New York: McGraw-Hill, 1964.

Pickford, R. W. 'Aesthetic, Technical Factors in Artistic Appreciation'. _British Journal of Psychology_, 38, 1948.

Seashore, C. E. _Psychology of Music_. New York: McGraw-Hill, 1938.

Smith, W. J. _Music in Education_. Faber and Faber, London, 1947.

Wing, H. D. 'Is Musical Aptitude Innate?'. _Review of Psychology of Music_, 1963 (Psychology Abstract, 1964, 10110).

Witkin, R. W. _The Intelligence of Feeling_. London: Heinemann, 1974.

Printed in Scotland by Her Majesty's Stationery Office at HMSO Press, Edinburgh
Dd 630260 K20 6/79 (16436)